Level 2 Diploma for IT Users
for City & Guilds

Presentation Graphics

for Office XP

Level
2

Rosemarie Wyatt

Endorsed by

**City&
Guilds**

www.heinemann.co.uk
✓ Free online support
✓ Useful weblinks
✓ 24 hour online ordering

01865 888058

Heinemann Educational Publishers
Halley Court, Jordan Hill, Oxford OX2 8EJ
Part of Harcourt Education

Heinemann is the registered trademark of
Harcourt Education Limited

Text © Rosemarie Wyatt 2004

First published 2004

08 07 06 05 04
10 9 8 7 6 5 4 3 2 1

British Library Cataloguing in Publication Data is available
from the British Library on request.

ISBN 0 435 46251 2

Publisher's note
The materials in this Work have been developed by Harcourt Education and the
content and accuracy are the sole responsibility of Harcourt Education. The City and
Guilds of London Institute accepts no liability howsoever in respect of any breach of
the intellectual property rights of any third party howsoever occasioned or damage
to the third party's property or person as a result of the use of this Work.

The City & Guilds name and logo are the registered trade marks of The City and
Guilds of London Institute and are used under licence.

Typeset by Tech Set Ltd
Printed by Thomson Litho Ltd

Acknowledgement
The publishers wish to acknowledge that the screenshots in this book have been
reprinted with kind permission from Microsoft Corporation

Contents

Introduction

This book assumes that you have acquired the skills and knowledge necessary for Presentation Graphics Level 1 and builds on those skills, introducing additional features such as Master slides, transition effects and timings. Instructions given are for the use of Microsoft PowerPoint 2002 and XP, though the City & Guilds unit is not specific and can be completed using any application and operating system.

The unit is organised into seven outcomes. You will learn to:

- create, save and use a new presentation/slideshow template
- add text to a presentation/slideshow from various sources, and control its attributes
- add graphics to a presentation/slideshow from various sources, and control its attributes
- add animation and multimedia objects to a presentation/slideshow
- modify existing text and graphics, separately and in combination
- produce hard copy from, and viewer versions of, a presentation/slideshow
- create, save and edit both a presentation controlled by a pointing device, and an automatically-timed slideshow.

The specific skills and underpinning knowledge for the outcomes of this Presentation Graphics unit are covered, although they are not dealt with by outcome or in the same order.

Each section covers several practical skills as well as underpinning knowledge related to the unit outcomes. This is followed by skills practice and a chance to check your knowledge. Consolidation tasks give you the opportunity to put together skills and knowledge, and a practice assignment complete your progress towards the actual assignment. As with all skills, practice makes perfect! Solutions to the skills practice, knowledge checks, consolidation and a practice assignment can be found at the back of the book.

Your tutor will give you a copy of the outcomes, as provided by City & Guilds, so that you can sign and date each learning point as you master the skills and knowledge.

There is often more than one way of carrying out a task in PowerPoint, e.g. using the toolbar, menu or keyboard. Whilst this book may use one method, there are others, and alternatives are listed at the back in the quick reference guide.

You will need several text documents to carry out certain tasks and the content for these can be found in the appendix, although your tutor may have prepared them for you. You will also need access to sources of image files and the internet or an intranet. The tasks are designed to be worked through in order, as earlier tasks may be used in later sections. Good luck!

Section 1 | Presentation graphics – basics

You will revise how to:

- Create a multi-slide presentation
- Add clip art
- Change slide order
- Change slide layout
- Save
- Open existing files
- Print in various formats

This book assumes that you have already acquired the skills and knowledge for Presentation Graphics Level 1, and as those topics will be familiar to you, you may be given brief reminders rather than full instructions. This section provides a chance to revise some of those features of PowerPoint. Check your knowledge boxes at the end of this section, and at the end of others, may include questions that test knowledge covered for Level 1, and will provide useful revision.

Information

PowerPoint uses **Slide Layouts** to help you set out a presentation in a consistent manner. Placeholders are displayed ready to hold text when keyed in, and are formatted to particular fonts and sizes. Objects such as headings will be in the same position on each slide, making a smoother presentation.

Task 1.1 | Create a presentation

Hint:

A Title slide is often used for the first slide of a presentation but it can be used at any stage.

Method

1 Load PowerPoint.
2 Normal View is displayed (Figure 1.1).

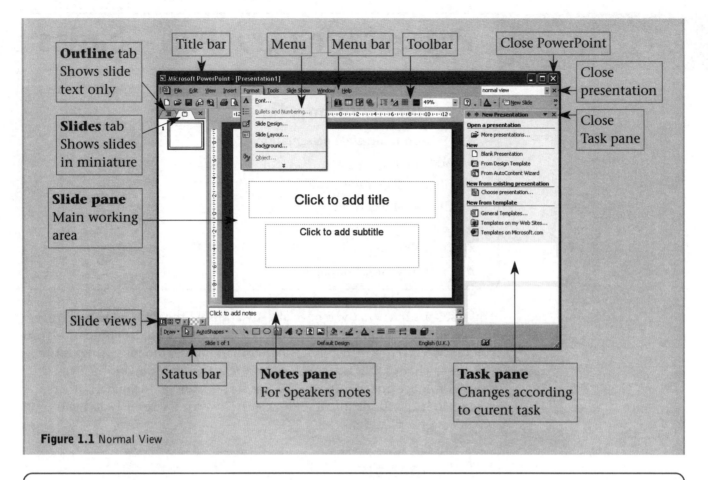

Figure 1.1 Normal View

Information: PowerPoint Normal View

- **Slide pane** – this is the main working area where you create slide content.
- **Outline tab/Slides tab** – you can alternate between the two tabs. Slide tab shows the slides as thumbnails. Outline tab shows text only – text can be entered and edited using this view.
- **Notes pane** – used for adding speaker's notes.
- **Task pane** – this changes according to the current task. To start with it offers choices for new presentations. The Task pane can be closed by clicking on ✕ in the top right corner of that pane (take care not to close the presentation).

Information

At this point it would be helpful to ensure that both the full standard and formatting toolbars are displayed. They may be displayed together in a single row (Figure 1.2).

Standard toolbar   Formatting toolbar

Figure 1.2 Toolbars

If they are, select **Customize** from the **Tools** menu and click on the **Options** tab. Check the option **Show Standard and Formatting toolbars on two rows** (Figure 1.3). Close.

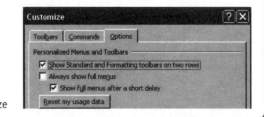

Figure 1.3 Customize

3 Click on the slide in the top placeholder **(Click to add title)** and key in **Applications Software**.

4 Click in the placeholder below **(Click to add subtitle)** and key in **An Introduction**.

5 Click on **Save** and accept the name **Applications Software** suggested.

6 Click on **New Slide** button. If this button is not visible, click on **Toolbar options** on the Formatting toolbar and select it – the button should then remain visible on the toolbar.

7 The Task pane changes to **Slide Layout** view (Figure 1.4) and a new **Title and Text** slide appears.

8 Click in the placeholder **Click to add title** and key in **Different types**.

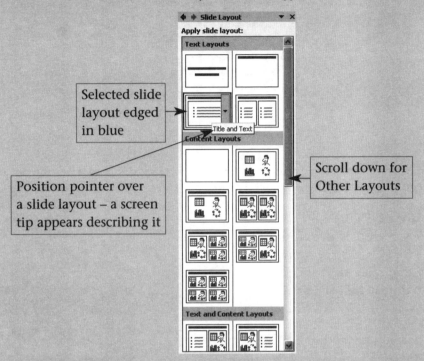

Selected slide layout edged in blue

Position pointer over a slide layout – a screen tip appears describing it

Scroll down for Other Layouts

Figure 1.4 Slide layout pane

Figure 1.5 Other Layouts – Title, Text and Clip Art

9 Click in the lower placeholder **Click to add text** and key in **Word Processing**.

10 Press **Enter** and key in **Spreadsheets**.

11 Press **Enter** and key in **Databases**.

12 Press **Enter** and key in **Desktop Publishing**.

13 Press **Enter** and key in **Presentation Graphics**.

14 Click on **New Slide** button, scroll down the Slide Layout task pane and choose the **Title, Text and Clip Art Layout** from **Other Layouts** (Figure 1.5).

15 Key in the title **Word Processing**.

16 Key in the list below. You will add clip art later.
- Working mainly with text
- Letters
- Memos
- Reports
- Lists
- Tables

17 Click on **New Slide** button ⠿ New Slide and choose **Title, Clip Art and Text** from **Other Layouts.**

18 Key in the title **Desktop Publishing**.

19 Key in the list below:

- Working with text and graphics
- Posters
- Leaflets
- Advertisements
- Newsletters
- Booklets

20 Click on **New Slide** button ⠿ New Slide and choose the **Title, Text and Clip Art** layout.

21 Key in the title **Spreadsheets**.

22 Key in the list below:

- Working with numbers
- Budgets
- Invoices
- Accounts
- Charts

23 Save the presentation.

Information: Moving around a presentation in the Slide pane

Using the keyboard (Figure 1.6)

Press **Page Up** key to display **previous** slide.
Press **Page Down** key to display **next** slide.
Press **Home** key to display **first** slide.
Press **End** key to display **last** slide.

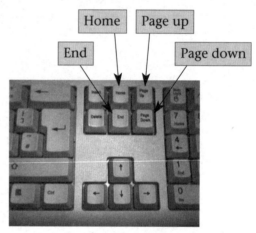

Figure 1.6 Moving around

Try each of these keys now.

Using the scroll bar (Figure 1.7)

Use the vertical scroll bar on the right of the window.

Click on the appropriate **single** arrow to move to **previous** or **next** slide.

Click on the **double** arrows to move to the **previous** or **next** slide.

Try each of these now.

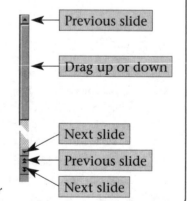

Figure 1.7 Scroll bar

Task 1.2   Insert clip art

Method

1   Move to the last slide titled **Spreadsheets** using one of the above methods.
2   In the slide window, double-click on the icon in the clip art placeholder
     (Figure 1.8). **Select Picture** window opens.
3   Key in **numbers** in the **Search text** box and click on **Search**. (Try
     calculator as an alternative search word if no images appear.)
4   Select an image from those offered, scrolling down if necessary.
5   Click OK – the image appears in the placeholder.

Figure 1.8 Add clip art

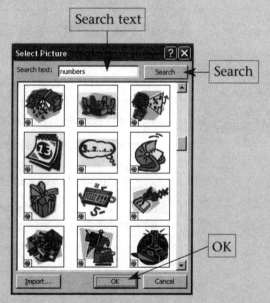

Figure 1.9 Select Picture

6   Move to the Word Processing slide and insert clip art, searching on the word
     letters or report.
7   Move to the Desktop Publishing slide and insert clip art of your choice. (Try
     book or **poster**.)
8   Save the presentation.

Information: Working in different views

Whilst Normal view is the usual way of working, remember that there are others. Try these now by clicking on the appropriate button in the bottom left corner of the window (Figure 1.10).

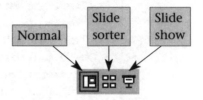

Figure 1.10 Slide views

1   The current view is **Normal View** ⬛. This is shown in Figure 1.1 and features the **Slide pane** – the main working area, **Notes pane** at the bottom and **Outline/Slides** tabs on the left.

2   Click on **Slide Sorter** view ⬛. This view provides an overview of all slides in miniature and can be used for changing the order of slides, adding and deleting slides.

3   Click on **Slide Show** view ⬛. This is used for viewing a presentation – each slide full screen. Press **Enter** to move from one slide to the next. Press **Esc** to stop (top left of keyboard).

The above views can also be found by selecting from the **View** menu. Try this now.

Hint:

You can also click the mouse to move through the slides.

Remember:

To drag the mouse means to hold the left button down and move the mouse.

Information: Changing slide order

To move a slide, drag it to its new position.

You can do this in **Slide Sorter** view by dragging on the slide. As you drag the mouse, a vertical line moves with it (Figure 1.11). When the mouse is released, the selected slide moves to that position.

To move a slide in **Normal View**, on the **Slides tab** drag a slide to a new position. A horizontal line indicates where the slide will be moved to. On the **Outline tab**, drag a slide icon to a new position.

It is probably more straightforward to use Slide Sorter view, especially when you have a lot of slides.

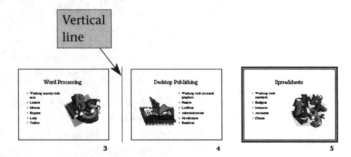

Figure 1.11 Change slide order

Task 1.3 — Change slide order

Method

1   Click on **Slide Sorter** view 🔲 .
2   Drag slide 5 (Spreadsheets) to a new position in front of Desktop Publishing. Ensure the vertical line that appears (Figure 1.11) is in the correct position before releasing the mouse.
3   Save the presentation.

Information: Changing slide layout

When you insert a new slide, you make a choice about its layout. Sometimes you may want to change the layout of an existing slide.

Task 1.4 — Change slide layout

Method

The Spreadsheet slide currently shows bulleted text on the left and clip art on the right. You are going to change this so the clip art is on the opposite side. Slide layout can be changed in any view.

1   Click on **Normal** view and select the **Spreadsheet** slide.
2   Click on **Format** menu and select **Slide Layout**.
3   Select **Title, Clip Art and Text** layout (Figure 1.12).

Remember:

A description of the slide layout appears when you select it.

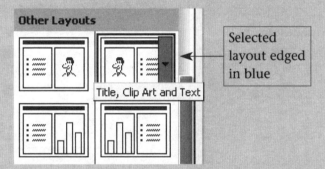

Figure 1.12 Change slide layout

4   Select the **Desktop Publishing** slide.
5   Click on **Format** menu and select **Slide Layout** as before.
6   Select **Title, Text and Clip Art** layout.
7   Save the presentation.

Information: Checking spelling

You should already be familiar with the spellcheck from Level 1. There will always be words that the spellcheck does not recognise, such as proper names, although you may use them frequently. These words appear with a red wavy line below but this does not necessarily mean that they are wrong. Any words you are likely to use again should be added to the dictionary and will then be ignored next time you check spelling. Whilst the spellcheck is very useful, you should always check your work by reading it through and checking it against the original text from which you are working. Use the spellcheck now by clicking on the spelling icon ABC. If you have not made any mistakes the Spelling dialogue box below (Figure 1.13) will not appear at this point. Refer back to it later when necessary.

Ignore	Ignores a word
Ignore All	Ignores a word each time it appears
Change	Changes a word to whatever appears in the Change to: box
Change All	Changes a word every time it appears
Add	Adds a word to the dictionary
Suggest	Gives a list of suggested spellings to select from

Figure 1.13 Check spelling

Task 1.5   Open existing presentation file

Before you start, close any presentations and close PowerPoint.

Method

1   Load PowerPoint.

Hint:

The **New presentation** task pane shows recently used files at the top of the list.

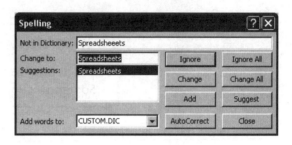

Figure 1.14 Open existing presentation file –Task pane

2   If the Task pane is displayed (Figure 1.14), select **Applications Software** from the list. If the file you want is not visible, click on **More presentations**, select the file from My Documents (Figure 1.15) and click **Open**.

If the Task pane is not visible, select **Open** from the **File** menu and select the presentation file **Applications Software** from My Documents (Figure 1.15).

Remember:

You can display the Task pane by selecting it from the **View** menu.

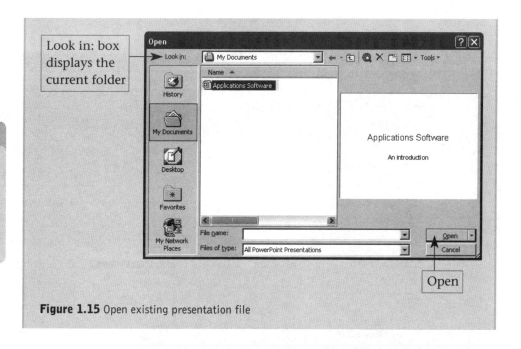

Look in: box displays the current folder

Remember:

When you are locating files stored in folders, double-click on the folder name so that the required folder is displayed in the Look in box.

Open

Figure 1.15 Open existing presentation file

Task 1.6 Print options

There are various ways of printing slides.

Slides. If you select the Print icon 🖨 the complete presentation will be printed, each slide filling a separate page.

Handouts. Handouts can be printed showing smaller versions of several slides. You can choose to print 1, 2, 3, 4, 6 or 9 to a page. Handouts can be useful to give to an audience as a reminder of your presentation. If you print three to a page, these are shown down the left-hand side of the page with the right-hand side left free for notes.

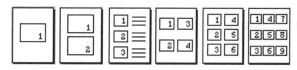

Figure 1.16 Handouts

Outline. An Outline printout shows only the text as seen in the Outline pane. Graphics, such as clip art and WordArt do not show, nor do text boxes you create yourself.

Method

1   To print all slides, one to a page, click on the **Print** button 🖨.
2   To print handouts, select **Print** from the **File** menu (Figure 1.17).

First select the **Print range** required – which slides you require to be printed.
Then select from **Print what** – how you want them to be printed.

3   Under **Print range**, select **All**.
4   Click on the down arrow under **Print what** and select **Handouts**.
5   Click on the down arrow by **Slides per page** and select **4**.
6   Click **OK**.

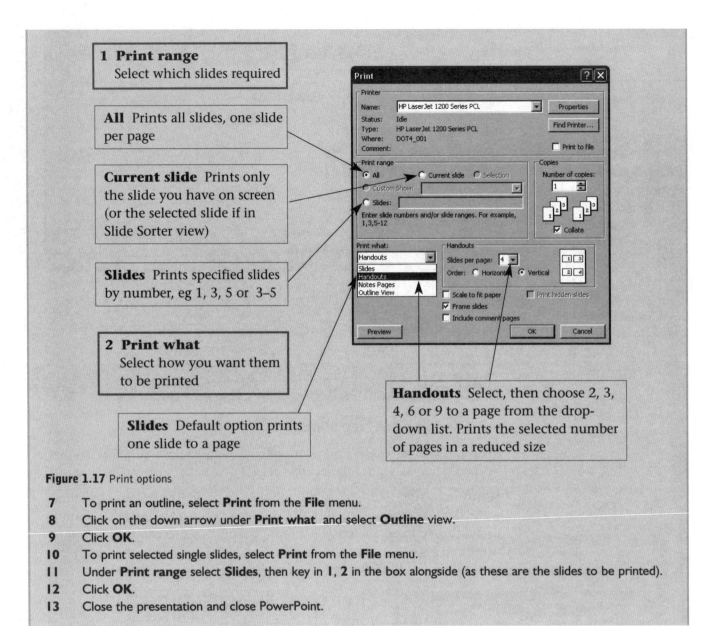

1 Print range
Select which slides required

All Prints all slides, one slide per page

Current slide Prints only the slide you have on screen (or the selected slide if in Slide Sorter view)

Slides Prints specified slides by number, eg 1, 3, 5 or 3–5

2 Print what
Select how you want them to be printed

Slides Default option prints one slide to a page

Handouts Select, then choose 2, 3, 4, 6 or 9 to a page from the drop-down list. Prints the selected number of pages in a reduced size

Figure 1.17 Print options

7   To print an outline, select **Print** from the **File** menu.
8   Click on the down arrow under **Print what** and select **Outline** view.
9   Click **OK**.
10   To print selected single slides, select **Print** from the **File** menu.
11   Under **Print range** select **Slides**, then key in **1, 2** in the box alongside (as these are the slides to be printed).
12   Click **OK**.
13   Close the presentation and close PowerPoint.

→ Practise your skills 1.1

1 Load PowerPoint and open the presentation **Applications Software**.
2 Move to the last slide and insert a new slide, selecting **Title, Clip Art and Text** layout.
3 Key in the heading **Databases**.
4 In the text placeholder below the heading, key in the list as follows:

   • **Storing and organising data**
   • **Searching**
   • **Sorting**
   • **Listing**
   • **Reporting**

5 Insert clip art on the left.

6 Add another new slide, selecting **Title, Text and Clip Art** layout.

7 Key in the heading **Presentation Graphics**.

8 Key in the list as follows:
- **For presenting information**
- **Text**
- **Images**
- **Shapes**
- **Effects**

9 Insert clip art on the right.

10 Change the order of the slides so that the slide **Databases** appears in front of **Desktop Publishing**.

11 Change the layout of the slides with clip art so that the clip art is on the right on all slides.

12 Insert a new Title slide at the end of the presentation.

13 In the title box, key in **Presented by**.

14 In the subtitle box key in your own name.

15 Click on **Slide Show** view 🖳 to view the presentation.

16 Check, save and print as handouts, nine to a page.

17 Print the slides 5 and 7 only as handouts, two to a page.

18 Close the presentation.

Hint:

To change more than one slide at once, hold the **Control** key down and click on each slide that needs to be selected.

Hint:

You can also view by selecting **Slide Show** from the **View** menu.

Hint:

Clicking on the **New** presentation icon 🗋, automatically loads a blank presentation with a Title slide.

Hint:

The lowercase **e** may change automatically to an uppercase **E**. Click **Undo** ↺ to revert to lowercase.

→ Practise your skills 1.2

1 Open a new blank presentation and select the **Title slide** layout.

2 Key in the title **City & Guilds**.

3 Key in the subtitle **e-Quals for IT Users**.

4 Save the presentation as **City & Guilds** now and save regularly as you work.

5 Insert a new slide selecting **Title, Text and Clip Art** layout.

6 Key in the title **Level 3 Advanced Diploma for IT Users**.

7 Key in the list below:
- **IT Principles**
- **Word Processing**
- **Spreadsheets**
- **Desk Top Publishing**
- **Integrated Applications**
- **Web Site Design**
- **Relational Databases**

8 Insert clip art on the right searching on the word **computer**.

9 Insert a new slide selecting **Title and 2-Column Text** layout (Figure 1.18).

Figure 1.18 Title and 2-Column Text layout

10 Key in the heading **Level 2 – Diploma for IT Users**.

11 In the left hand text column key in the following:
- **Word Processing**
- **Spreadsheets**
- **Databases**
- **Using the Internet**
- **Presentation Graphics**
- **Computerised Accounts**

12 In the right-hand column key in the following:
- **Desk Top Publishing**
- **Integrated Applications**
- **Multi media**
- **Web Site Design**

13 Insert a new slide selecting **Title, Text and Clip Art** layout.

14 Key in the title **Level 1 – Certificate for IT Users**.

15 Key in the bulleted list as follows:
- **IT Principles**
- **Word Processing**
- **Spreadsheets**
- **Databases**
- **Using the Internet**
- **Presentation Graphics**
- **E-Mail**
- **Desk Top Publishing**

16 Insert suitable clip art on the right of the slide.

17 Proofread and spellcheck the presentation.

18 Save the presentation and print handouts, four to a page.

19 Change the layout of the two slides with clip art so that the image is on the left.

20 Change the order of the slides so that following the first slide, Level 1, Level 2 and Level 3 appear in that order.

21 Switch back to Normal view and insert a new Title slide.

22 In the title box, key in **Presented by**.

23 In the subtitle box key in your own name.

24 This new slide should be positioned at the end of the presentation. Move it now if necessary, in Slide Sorter view.

25 Save the presentation as **City & Guilds Version 2**, selecting **Save As** from the **File** menu.

26 Click on **Slide Show** view 🖥 to view the presentation, pressing **Enter** to move through the slides.

27 Print as handouts, six to a page.

28 Print an Outline view.

29 Close the presentation and close PowerPoint.

Remember:

Using Save As allows you save a presentation with a new name, but keeping the original intact.

Note:

Handouts printed three to a page display lines for handwritten notes.

→ Check your knowledge

1 What are Slide Layouts?

2 How can Slide Layouts help to ensure consistency throughout a presentation?

3 How can you change a layout once you have created a slide?

4 State two ways of changing from Slide Sorter view to Normal view.

5 In Slide Sorter view, how can you select more than one slide?

In order to create professional-looking presentations it is important that all slides have a consistent style. In the previous section you used Slide Layouts and now you will use a Slide Master.

Information: Master slides

Whilst Slide Layouts are used for a consistent layout throughout a presentation with the use of placeholders, the Master slide is used to set the style for the font, font size and colour, as well as the position and size of the placeholders upon which each slide is based. Changes made will be applied automatically to existing slides and to any new slides. Background colours can be chosen and logos and graphics can also be placed on the master to display on every slide.

Task 2.1 | Set up a Master slide

Method

1 Load PowerPoint and open the presentation **Applications Software**.
2 Click on **View** menu and select **Master**, then **Slide Master** from the side menu (Figure 2.1). The Slide Master appears (Figure 2.2).

Figure 2.1 Select Slide Master

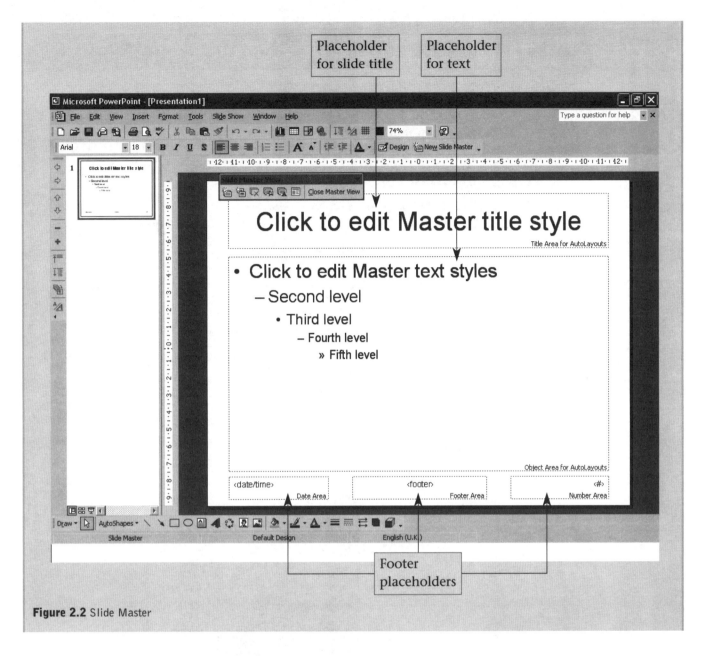

Figure 2.2 Slide Master

Notice the placeholders that make up the Master slide. These are used to format the text that will appear in them on each slide.

Master title style. Click in this placeholder to change font, alignment, colour etc. for all slide titles.

Master text styles. Formatting for bulleted text can be changed here in the same way. It is also possible to change bullet styles. The Second and Third levels etc. referred to, relate to sub-bullets, which are dealt with later.

Footer. There are three footer placeholders, for the date and/or time, slide numbering, as well as for any personalised footer text (e.g. your name) that you may require.

Any of these placeholders can be moved.

Apart from text formatting, the slide master can be used for applying other features to all slides, for example, applying background colours, changing bullet styles and adding clip art. You will start using the master in the next task and apply a background colour.

Task 2.2   Apply a background

A background is a colour, pattern or picture applied to give interest to the slides. It should not affect the readability of the text so you should be careful when making your choice.

Method

1   Select **Background** from the **Format** menu.
2   Click on the down arrow and select **More Colors** (Figure 2.3).

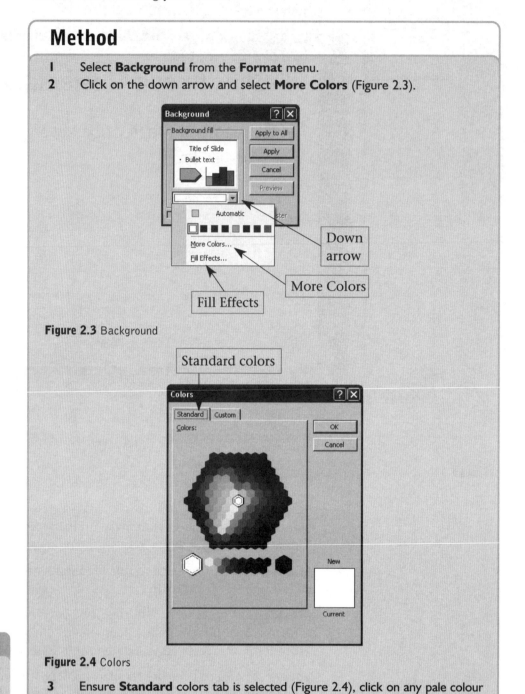

Figure 2.3 Background

Figure 2.4 Colors

3   Ensure **Standard** colors tab is selected (Figure 2.4), click on any pale colour and click **OK**.
4   Click on **Apply to All**.

Hint:

You can apply a background to a single slide by clicking **Apply** rather than **Apply to All**.

Task 2.3 — Create a gradient fill effect background

A gradient fill involves the blending of two colours or shades together. You will blend the original colour chosen with a second colour.

Method

I	Select **Background** from the **Format** menu.
2	Click on the down arrow and select **Fill Effects** (Figure 2.3).
3	Select **Two colors** (Figure 2.5).

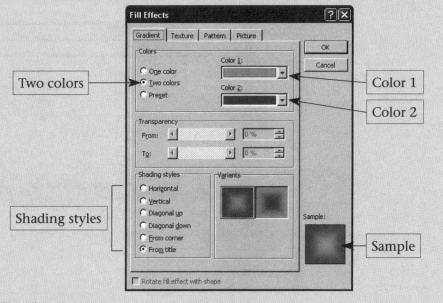

Figure 2.5 Gradient fill

Note:

Notice how colours previously chosen appear in the colour scheme.

4	**Color I** will stay as your original colour. Click on the down arrow next to **Color 2**. Choose a colour from **More colors**.
5	Note the variety of **Shading styles**, try them and see the effect in the Sample.
6	Finally, choose **From title**.
7	Click **OK**.
8	Choose **Apply to All**.

Task 2.4 — Save to a new file creating a new folder

In order to preserve the original presentation, you will now save this new version to a new folder with a different name using **Save As**.

Method

I	Select **Save As** from the **File** menu (Figure 2.6).
2	Click on **Create new folder** and key in the folder name **Presentation Graphics Level 2**.

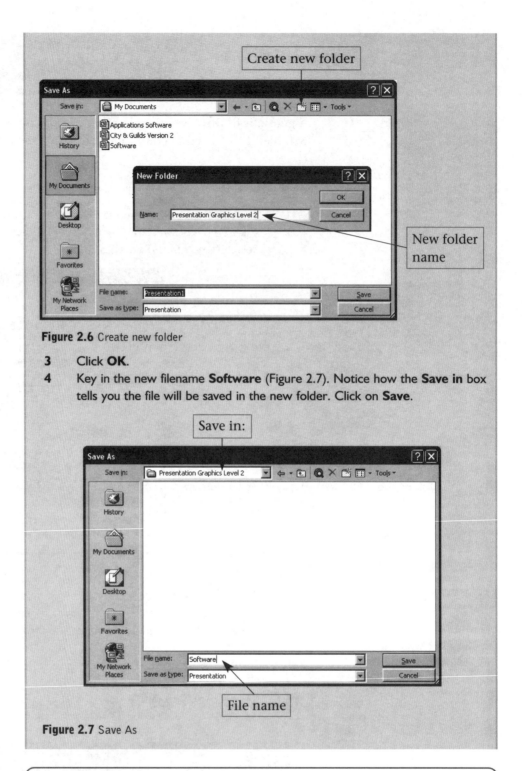

Figure 2.6 Create new folder

3 Click **OK**.

4 Key in the new filename **Software** (Figure 2.7). Notice how the **Save in** box tells you the file will be saved in the new folder. Click on **Save**.

Figure 2.7 Save As

Information: Text attributes

Default attributes refer to the automatic settings for text style, e.g. Times New Roman size 20. The default font size for a Master slide title is 44, with Master text size of 32. This is much larger than text found in a word processed document because slides do not contain a lot of text and are normally shown on a large screen. As the audience may be viewing from a distance it is important that the text is clear and large enough to read. Fancy fonts would not be a good choice. Text colours should be chosen with care to ensure slides can be read easily, particularly when a coloured background is used.

| Task 2.5 | Change default text attributes |

Figure 2.8 shows some formatting features you should already be familiar with.

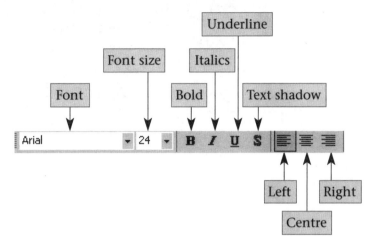

Figure 2.8 Font style and alignment

Method

1   Click in the title placeholder (Figure 2.2).
2   Click on the dropdown arrow beside the font name (Figure 2.8) and select **Tahoma** (or Arial if not available).
3   Now click on the dropdown arrow beside the font size box and select **40**.
4   Click on the **Shadow** icon.
5   Click on **Left align**.

To change font colour you will use the **Drawing toolbar** (Figure 2.9). If this toolbar is not displayed at the bottom of the screen, select **Toolbars** from the **View** menu, and **Drawing** from the side menu that appears.

Figure 2.9 Drawing toolbar

6   Click on the dropdown arrow beside the **Font Color** button **A ▾** and click on **More colors** as you did for background colour. Select a dark colour and click **OK**.
7   Click in the placeholder labelled **Click to edit Master text styles** and choose the same font, **Tahoma**, and size **32** (the default size).

Notice how only one line changes. To change all bullet levels, highlight all text in the placeholder first (the bullets themselves will not appear to be highlighted).

8   Change the font colour of this placeholder.
9   Save the presentation.

Task 2.6 — Change bullet style

Method

1 Click in the first line of the Master text styles (the first bullet point).
2 Select **Bullets and Numbering** from the **Format** menu (Figure 2.10).
3 Select a **bullet style** and click **OK**.
4 Save.

Hint:

If you are using more than one level of bullets, highlight them all before selecting a bullet style.

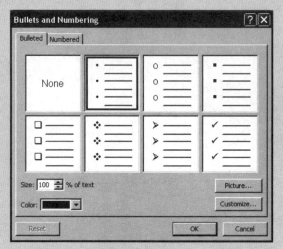

Figure 2.10 Change bullet style

Task 2.7 — Format placeholder fill colour

Method

1 Click in the Title placeholder.
2 Click on the dropdown arrow beside the **Fill Color** button on the Drawing toolbar (Figure 2.9) and choose **More fill colors**.
3 Choose a colour and click **OK**.
4 Save.

Hint:

You can also change colour by selecting **Placeholder** from the **Format** menu.

Task 2.8   Insert clip art and resize

In the last section you inserted clip art using a layout placeholder. Here you will place a small image as a logo without using a placeholder.

Method

I   Select **Picture** from the **Insert** menu and choose **Clip Art** from the side menu. The Insert Clip Art task pane appears (Figure 2.11).

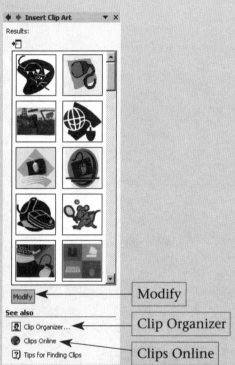

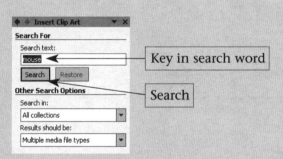

Figure 2.11 Insert Clip Art task pane

Figure 2.12 Select clip art

2   Key in the word **mouse** in the Search text: box and click on **Search**. A list of images appears (Figure 2.12).
3   Click on an image to select it (choose a computer mouse!).
4   Resize the image by dragging a corner handle inwards towards the middle, to make it smaller. The pointer changes to a diagonal double-headed arrow ↖ (Figure 2.13).
5   Now move the image to the top left-hand corner of the slide by positioning the pointer in the middle of the image and dragging. The pointer changes to the four-headed Move icon ✛.

Figure 2.13 Resize clip art

Sometimes you may be required to resize an object by using precise measurements.

Method

1   Click on the image to select it.
2   Choose **Picture** from the **Format** menu.

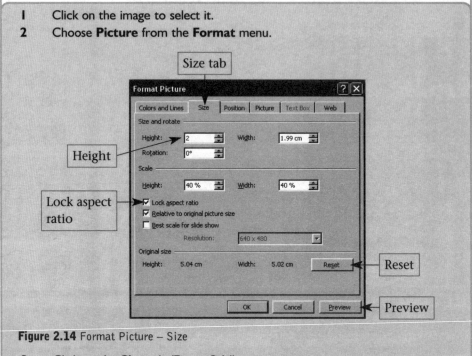

Figure 2.14 Format Picture – Size

3   Click on the **Size** tab (Figure 2.14).
4   Key in **1.5** cm in the height box.
5   Ensure there is a tick by **Lock aspect ratio** – this ensures the image will stay in its original proportion and not become distorted. Therefore you do not need a width measurement. Notice you can resize by a percentage.
6   Click on **Preview** to see how the image will look and then click **OK**.
7   Save.

Hint:

You can also click on **Reset** to restore the image to its original size, and **Cancel** if you want to cancel the current changes.

Information: Headers and footers

Headers and footers are items of information included at the top or bottom of a page. In PowerPoint you have the option of including the date, page number and text in the footer area of a slide.

Method

I   Select **Header and Footer** from the **View** menu.

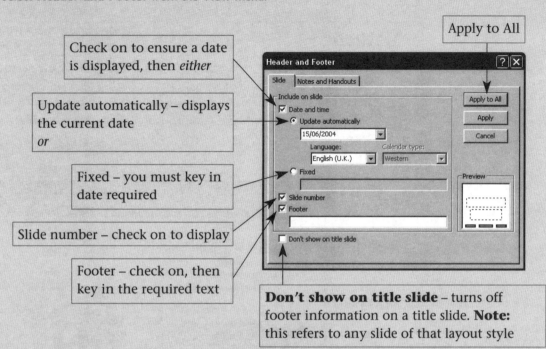

Apply to All

Check on to ensure a date is displayed, then *either*

Update automatically – displays the current date
or

Fixed – you must key in date required

Slide number – check on to display

Footer – check on, then key in the required text

Don't show on title slide – turns off footer information on a title slide. **Note:** this refers to any slide of that layout style

Figure 2.15 Add footer items

2   See Figure 2.15. A tick should be present for each item required. Tick the following:
Date and time
Update automatically (choose a date style from the dropdown list)
Slide number
Footer
3   In the footer box, key in your name.
4   Click on the option **Don't show on title slide**. (This means any slide that is of the Title layout, not necessarily just the first.)
5   Click **Apply to All**.
6   Click on or into the **Date Area** placeholder and change the font to **Tahoma** and the same colour as the main text.
7   Repeat for the **Footer Area** and **Number Area** placeholder.
8   Save.
9   Click on **View** menu and select **Normal.** Move through the slides to view the results of all these changes.

Note:

There are a variety of date styles to choose from – short and long dates, and time options.

Note:

You can add footers when working on a single slide by choosing **Apply** (to the current slide) rather than **Apply to All**.

Task 2.11 — Modify the slide number

You may need to include the number of slides in a presentation, for example slide 1 of 7. In the Number Area placeholder, <#> represents the page number.

Method

1   Switch back to the Master slide. Select **Master** from the **View** menu and **Slide Master** from the side menu.
2   In the **Number Area** placeholder, key in **Slide** in front of <#> and **of 8** after, to read **Slide** <#> **of 8**, remembering to leave a space before and after <#>.

Task 2.12 — Change Master slide layout

The size and position of any of the placeholders can be changed and they can also be deleted.

Method

1   Click in the **Date Area** and press **Delete**.
2   Click over the **Footer Area**. When the Move icon appears ⊕, drag the placeholder to the top of the slide.
3   To restore the Date Area, select **Master Layout** from the **Format** menu.
4   Click on **Date** and click **OK** (Figure 2.16).
5   Switch to **Slide Sorter** view ▦ and view the slides.

Figure 2.16 Master Layout

Information: Title Master

As you have seen, any formatting you apply to the Master slide affects all slides. It is also possible to use a Title Master to which different formatting can be applied. Any slide in the presentation that has a Title slide layout will take on this formatting. (A Title slide does not necessarily have to be only the first slide in a presentation.) You must be in Master Slide view before inserting a Title Master.

Task 2.13 Insert a Title Master

Method

1. Select **Master** from the **View** menu and then **Slide Master**.
2. Select **New Title Master** from the **Insert** menu.
3. Click in the title placeholder and change its fill colour. (Use the **Fill Color** button  ▾ on the Drawing toolbar.)
4. Centre the text in the title placeholder.
5. Notice how you switch between the Master and the Title Master using the slide miniatures on the left of the screen (Figure 2.17).
6. Switch to **Slide Sorter** view and notice how the two Title slides are formatted differently from the other slides.
7. Save and print as handouts, nine to a page.
8. Close the presentation.

Figure 2.17 Switch between Master views

Task 2.14 Open a presentation from a different folder

You are going to open **City & Guilds Version 2** which you saved directly into **My Documents**.

Method

1. Select **Open** from the **File** menu.
2. In Figure 2.18, the current folder is Presentation Graphics Level 2. Click on **My Documents**. The current folder will change.
3. Select **City & Guilds Version 2** and click on **Open**. You will use this presentation for the next task.

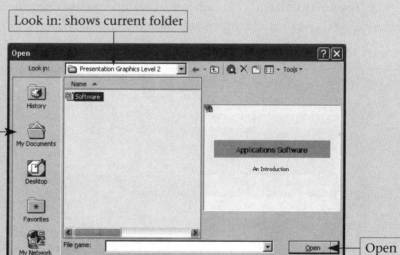

Look in: shows current folder

My Documents

Open

Figure 2.18 Open existing presentation

Remember:

If the folder you require is not displayed in the **Look in** box, click on **My Documents** in the left sidebar to find a list of all your folders.

Remember:

You can always double-click on a filename to open it.

Information: Additional sources of clip art

Clip art can also be selected using options at the bottom of the Insert Clip Art task pane (Figure 2.12) – the **Clip Organizer** (where clip art is stored in categories) and **Clips Online**. Open a new presentation and experiment now.

Clicking on **Clip Organizer** shows the Collection List of clip art as seen on the left of Figure 2.19. The + beside **Office Collections** indicates there are sub folders – clicking on + shows them. If you click on a folder you will see the images inside. Sometimes sub folders have even more folders inside them. Select an image and click on its side bar. Choose **Copy** and then click onto the slide window before pasting the clip art image onto the slide.

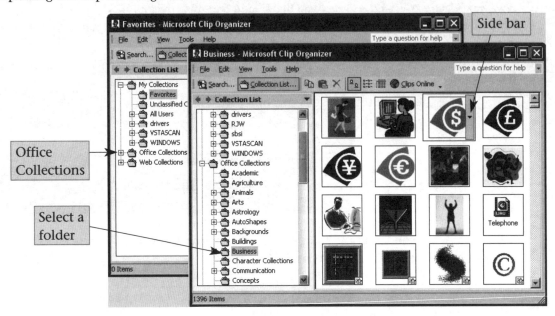

Figure 2.19 Clip Organizer

Using the Internet is beyond the scope of this book but if you have an Internet connection, clicking on **Clips Online** leads to the Microsoft website where there are more collections that you can search through. Clip art can be copied and pasted in the same way as described above.

Close the presentation without saving when you have finished experimenting.

→ Practise your skills 2.1

1 Using **City & Guilds Version 2**, switch to the master page.

2 Apply a two-colour **gradient fill effect background** with the shading style **From corner**.

3 Format the background of the title placeholder with one of the chosen colours.

4 Change the Master title style font to **Arial** size **40**, **italics** and aligned to the right.

5 Change the Master text style to **Arial**.

6 Insert a clip art image of a computer and resize it to a width of 3 cm, keeping aspect ratio.

7 Position the image above the number area in the bottom right corner of the Master slide. Check on the slides themselves to ensure the image is not obscured by text. Adjust its position if necessary.

8 Insert the date to update automatically choosing a month and year style, eg October 04.

9 Include the slide number.

10 Add the footer text **www.e-quals.co.uk**.

11 Footer information is not required to display on the Title slide.

12 Modify the page number to read **Page <#> of 4**.

13 Insert a Title Master.

14 Left align and embolden the text in the title placeholder.

15 Save the presentation as **City & Guilds Version 3** to a new folder called **Skills Practice Level 2**.

16 Print the presentation as handouts, six to a page.

17 Move the footer text to the top middle of the slide.

18 Delete the date placeholder.

19 Print slide 1 as a single slide.

20 Check the contents carefully.

21 View the presentation, save and close.

→ Check your knowledge

1 What is the purpose of a Master slide?

2 What should you consider when choosing background colours?

3 What should you consider when selecting text font, font sizes, colour and style?

4 What is the purpose of locking aspect ratio when resizing objects such as images?

5 What are the two options for including the date in a slide footer?

Consolidation 1

1 Open a new presentation with a Title slide.

2 Key in **Smarts Driving School** as the title (no sub-title).

3 Save as **Smarts Driving School** into a new folder called **Presentation Graphics Consolidation** folder. (**NOTE:** Ensure the **Save in** box reads My Documents before creating the new folder.)

4 Insert another Title slide and key in **High achievement rates** as the title and **Friendly instructors** as the sub-title.

5 The next four slides are **Title, Text and Clip Art** layout.

Services

- Driving lessons
- Intensive courses
- Theory preparation
- Practice tests
- Advanced driving
- Motorway driving
- Refresher courses

Practice tests

- Practice tests with different instructors
- All local test routes covered

Intensive courses

- One week all day
- Two weeks half day
- Individual programmes
- Test at the end

Theory preparation

- Theory classroom sessions
- Computer-based practice
- Practice tests

6 The final slide is the **Title and Text** layout.

Other courses

- Advanced driving – preparation for the Advanced driving test
- Motorway driving – minimum two half day sessions
- Refresher courses – for those whose driving is a little rusty

7 Insert suitable clip art onto slides 3–6.

8 Switch to the Master slide and choose a **two-colour gradient fill effect** for the background with **From corner** shading style.

9 Change the Master title font to **Helvetica** or **Arial**, **bold** size **40** and **right align.**

10 Change the Master text font to the same.

11 Change the bullet style to one of your choice.

12 Add a footer to include the date and your name in the middle but no slide number.

13 The footer should not display on the Title slide.

14 Insert a **Title Master** and use a colour to fill the title placeholder.

15 Change the title text to **left align**.

16 Insert a clip art image of a car on the Title Master and size it to approximately **3 cm** wide.

17 Organise the order of the last five slides as follows:

Services

Intensive courses

Theory preparation

Practice tests

Other courses

18 Change the slide layout of slides 3–6 to **Title, Clip Art and Text**.

19 Proofread carefully and spellcheck.

20 Save and print as handouts, nine to a page.

21 Print an Outline view.

22 Close.

Templates

You will learn to:

- Apply a design template
- Create and use a template

Templates feature in many programs. They are yet another way of ensuring consistency and saving time. Whereas a Master slide forms the basis of all slides in a single presentation, a template is a master for new presentations that can be used over and over again. PowerPoint has many templates to select from, or you can create your own.

Information: Design templates

PowerPoint design templates each have their own colour scheme and decorative graphics. The designs include background colours, fonts, font colours and bullet styles. If applied to an existing presentation the new design overwrites any formatting applied to the Master slides. However, you can still access the Master slides and customise them if you wish.

Task 3.1 | Apply a design template

Method

1. Open **Smarts Driving School** from the **Presentation Graphics Consolidation** folder.
2. Select **Slide Design** from the **Format** menu (Figure 3.1) which opens the Slide Design task pane (Figure 3.2).

Figure 3.1 Slide Design

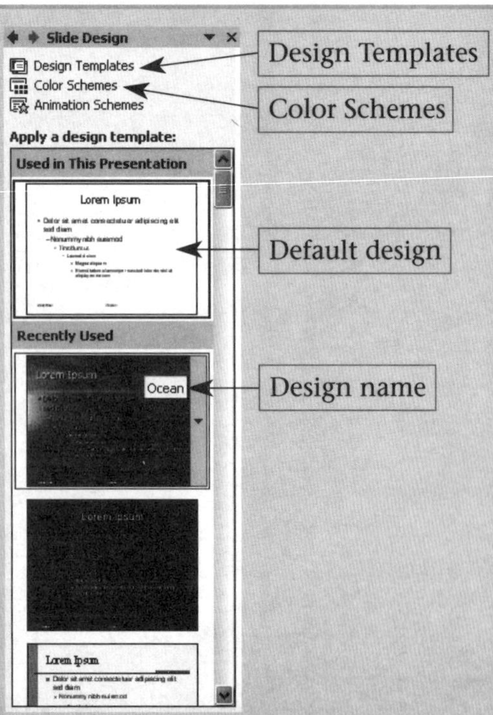

Figure 3.2 Slide Design task pane

3	Scroll up and down the list of templates and choose a design.
4	Move through the slides to see the effects of the design. Notice the colour scheme for text.
5	Try applying a different design template. Position the pointer on a design and its name appears.
6	Save as **Smarts Driving School Version 2**.

Hint:

The colour scheme can be changed by selecting **Colour Schemes** from the top of the task pane. Select **Design Templates** to return to design.

Task 3.2   Remove a design template

Method

I	If the Slide Design task pane is not open select **Slide Design** from the **Format** menu.
2	Scroll to the **Default Design** template and click on it to select.
3	Save and close.

Hint:

Position pointer on a design and its name appears.

Information: Templates

In any program a template is a file that is set up with layout and formatting in place, and in many cases particular information that you may wish to use over and over again. In PowerPoint we have already discussed design templates. You can, however, create templates yourself from scratch, choosing your own colours and styles, or you can adapt an existing design. You can also add text or graphics to a template so that it is already in place when you come to use it. For example, if you produce presentations regularly, you could include the same footer information every time, or your company name and logo. Some organisations may have templates for presentations with their own house style that everyone must use to ensure consistency and a professional effect. This might include a company logo and the use of particular fonts and colours.

Task 3.3   Create a design template

In this task you will create a template for Hill Oak Nursery.

Hint:

Select **Background** from the **Format** menu.

Hint:

Select **Bullets and Numbering** from the **Format** menu.

Hint:

Select **Header and Footer** from the **View** menu.

Method

I	Open a new blank presentation.
2	Switch to the Master slide and format the title and the text style font (bulleted text) to **Tempus Sans** and a dark green colour. If you do not have this font available, choose **Arial**.
3	Format the background with a **gradient** fill of two colours – **light yellow** and **light green** with the shading style **From title**.
4	Change the bullet style to one of your choice.
5	Insert footer information to display the date, the page number and the name **Hill Oak Nursery**. (If you are sharing a printer, also add your initials in brackets to distinguish your printouts from those of others.)

Hint:

Select **Picture** from the **Insert** menu and then **Clip Art**.

Hint:

Select **New Title Master** from the **Insert** menu.

6   Insert clip art searching on the word **oak** or **tree**. Resize it to a height of 1.5 cm, locking aspect ratio, and position it in the top right-hand corner.

7   Insert a new **Title Master**.

8   Change the shading style of the Title Master background to **Horizontal** – take care to use **Apply**, not Apply to All.

9   Select the image and click on **Copy** 📑.

10   With the Title master still selected, click on **Paste** 📋.

11   Move the copy to the opposite corner.

12   Click on **Paste** 📋 again and move the pasted image in the middle of the slide above the title.

13   Increase the height of the third image to **3 cm**, locking aspect ratio. Adjust its position if necessary.

14   Switch to **Normal view** 📇.

15   On the Title slide, click in the placeholder **Click to add title** and key in **Hill Oak Nursery**.

The template is now ready to be saved. It is important to check your work carefully including the use of the spellcheck. If you do not, any mistakes that have been made will appear every time the template is used.

16   Select **Save As** from the **File** menu.

17   In the **File name** box, key in **Hill Oak Nursery** (see Figure 3.3).

18   Click on the dropdown arrow alongside the **Save as type** box and select **Design Template**. Notice how the Save in box now reads **Templates** – PowerPoint automatically saves templates to a special folder.

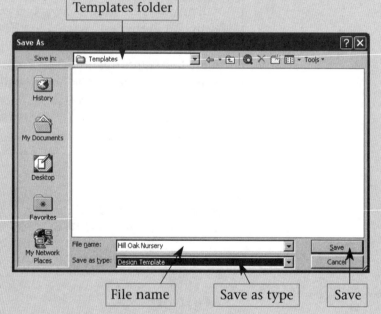

Figure 3.3 Save as a template

19   Click on **Save**.

20   Now close the presentation template.

Information

A file extension is the last part of a filename, preceded by a dot, e.g. Driving School.ppt. You may not be aware of file extensions as they are not always visible, but they give an indication of the file type, which in this case is a PowerPoint presentation. A PowerPoint template is saved automatically with the file extension .pot whereas a normal presentation has the extension .ppt.

| Task 3.4 | Use a copy of a template |

Method

Hint:

Notice that from this view you can also select the Design Templates tab and choose one of the designs you used in Task 3.1.

1   Select **New** from the **File** menu.
2   Click on **General Templates** in the New Presentation task pane (Figure 3.4).

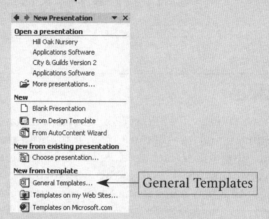

Figure 3.4 General Templates

3   Select **Hill Oak Nursery** from the list offered (Figure 3.5) and click **OK**.

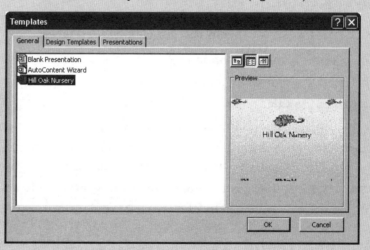

Figure 3.5 Templates

> **Note:** Opening a template in this way, opens a **copy** of the original.
> Notice the name in the title bar at the top of the screen, e.g. Presentation 2.

4   Click in the subtitle placeholder and key in **Conservatories and Leisure Buildings**.
5   Insert a new **Title, Text and Clip Art** slide and key in the title **Conservatories**.

6 Key in the list as follows:

- **Hardwood**
- **UPVC**
- **Self-build**
- **Full construction**
- **Furniture**
- **Blinds**

7 Insert suitable clip art.

8 Insert a new **Title, Text and Clip Art** slide and key in the title **Leisure Buildings**.

9 Key in the list as follows

- **Summerhouses**
- **Play houses**
- **Log cabins**
- **Greenhouses**
- **Garages**

10 Insert suitable clip art.

11 Use **Save As** from the **File** menu to save the presentation as **Hill Oak Buildings** into the **Presentation Graphics Level 2** folder.

12 Check your work carefully and view the presentation.

13 Print as handouts, three to a page.

14 Close the presentation.

Information

In Task 3.3 above you saw that PowerPoint saves templates to a templates folder. If you need to amend an original template you must open it up from this folder. Its location on your computer will vary – ask your tutor. It is in fact possible to save a template file to any folder of your choice just as you can with any other file. If you do this, when you come to use it it does not automatically open as a copy. Save it with a new name using Save As, leaving the original intact.

→ Practise your skills 3.1

In this task you will create a template for Park House Travel.

1 Open a new blank presentation.

2 Switch to the slide master and change the font throughout to one of your choice.

3 Left align the title.

4 Format the background with a **two-colour gradient** with a **diagonal up** shading style.

5 Insert a footer to show the date so that it updates automatically, the slide number, and your initials. The footer is not required on the Title slide.

6 Insert a clip art image searching on the word **globe** or **travel**.

7 Format the clip art image to a height of **2 cm**, locking aspect ratio, and position it in the top right corner.

8 Insert a Title Master and centre the Master title text.

9 Insert the same clip art image and enlarge it to a height of **4 cm** and position it above the title.

10 Switch to **Normal view** and on the Title slide key in the heading **Park House Travel**.

11 Save as a **Design template** with the name **Park House Travel**. (Remember that templates save automatically into a templates folder.)

12 Close the presentation template.

→ Practise your skills 3.2

Now you will use the new template.

1 Click on **New** from the **File** menu and select the template created above.

2 Key in the subtitle **Holidays and Services**.

3 Insert a new **Title, Text and Clip Art** slide.

4 Key in the title **Holidays**.

5 Key in the list:

- **Coach tours**
- **All-in packages**
- **Escorted tours**
- **Two centre holidays**
- **Activity holidays**
- **Weekend breaks**

6 Insert clip art searching on the word **beach**.

7 Insert a new **Title, Text and Clip Art** slide.

8 Key in the title **Services**.

9 Key in the list:

- **Flights only**
- **Insurance**
- **Foreign currency**
- **Car hire**
- **Doorstep pick-up**

10 Insert clip art searching on the word **plane**.

11 Proofread and spellcheck.

12 View the presentation.

13 Save the file as **Park House Holidays and Services** into the **Skills Practice Level 2** folder.

14 Print as handouts, three to a page.

15 Close the presentation.

→ Check your knowledge

1 What is a design template?

2 Why is it particularly important to check a template before saving it?

3 What are the advantages of using a template?

4 What are the benefits of a house style template when creating presentations?

5 What are the file extensions of a PowerPoint presentation and of a template?

Working with text

You will learn to:

- Use graphical text (WordArt)
- Insert text boxes
- Use rulers and guides

You have already inserted text into presentations in predefined positions using Slide Layouts. Sometimes you may need to position text yourself and text boxes will allow you to do this. Graphical text is another way of displaying text and can be used to add variety to a presentation.

Information: Graphical text

Graphical text can be inserted into a presentation using the WordArt feature. It might be used to draw attention to text and give interest to a slide. It is not always appropriate for a presentation and would depend on the audience and the subject.

Ensure the Drawing toolbar is displayed at the bottom of the screen. If it is not, select **Toolbars** from the **View** menu and then **Drawing**.

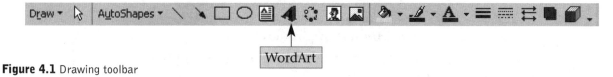

Figure 4.1 Drawing toolbar

Task 4.1   Insert WordArt, resize, move and edit

Method

1   Open a new blank presentation and using a Title slide, key in the title **Working with text**.
2   Insert a new **Blank slide** (Figure 4.2).

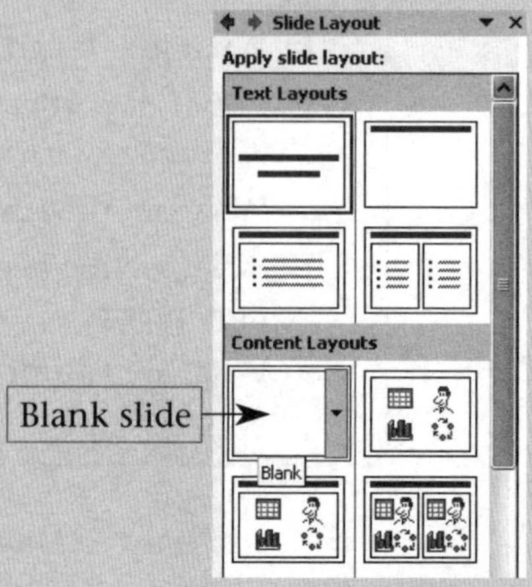

Figure 4.2 Blank slide

3   Click on the WordArt icon – the WordArt Gallery appears (Figure 4.3).

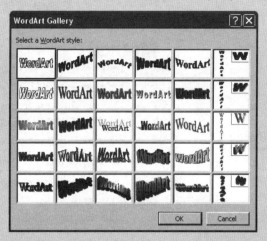

Figure 4.3 WordArt Gallery

4   Select a WordArt style and click **OK**.

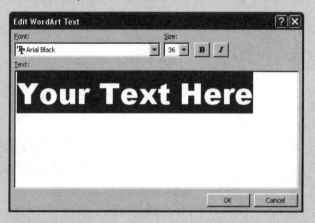

Figure 4.4 Enter WordArt

5   Key in **City and Guilds** to replace *Your Text Here* (Figure 4.4) and click **OK**.
6   Save as **Working with text** into the **Presentation Graphics Level 2** folder.
7   To resize WordArt, click on it to select it and drag a handle towards or away from the middle of the WordArt. Experiment with it. The adjust handle (the little yellow diamond) can be moved from side to side to slant it. The rotate handle (the green circle) can be used to rotate it.
8   To move WordArt, position the pointer over the words themselves and when the Move icon ⊕ appears, drag the WordArt to the top of the slide.
9   To edit WordArt, double-click on it. Delete **and** and key in **&** to replace it. Click **OK**.
10   Create more WordArt using the text **Presentation Graphics**. Position this at the bottom of the slide.
11   Save the presentation.

Hint:

Notice you can also select a different font and size.

Information: Text boxes

So far you have entered text into the placeholders that appear on Slide Layouts. If text is needed outside those areas you need to create a text box. The simplest way of creating a text box is simply to select the **Text box** button and click onto the slide.

Task 4.2 — Insert a text box, resize and move

Method

1. Click on the **Text box** button 🔳.
2. Click on the slide in between the two WordArt objects.
3. Key in **Unit 026: Level 2**.
4. **To move** the text box, position the pointer over the border (avoid the handles) of the text frame, until the Move icon ✛ appears. Move it approximately to the middle of the slide. In the next task you will position it accurately.
5. Save the presentation.

Hint:

Notice how the text box grows as the text is keyed in.

Hint:

Notice that the text in text boxes created by you does not appear in the Outline pane.

Hint:

PowerPoint does not have fixed margins and space right up to the edge of a slide can be used. Guides can be used if you require a specific space around the edge.

Information: Rulers and guides

Rulers and guides are often featured in software packages to position objects accurately on the page. PowerPoint also has this facility which can also be used for positioning images and other objects which you may use in later sections.

Task 4.3 — Use rulers and guides

Method

1. If the rulers across the top of the slide window and down the left side are not displayed, turn them on by selecting **Ruler** from the **View** menu.
2. To display guides, select **Grid and Guides** from the **View** menu and check on **Display grid** and **Display drawing guides** (Figure 4.5). The guides are shown across and down the middle of the slide lining up with the zero markers on the rulers.

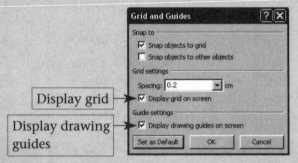

Figure 4.5 Grid and Guides

3. Click inside the text box so the cursor is flashing. Notice how the rulers display the width and height of the text box.
4. Click on the edge of the text box and notice how the guides are lined up with the zero markers on the ruler.
5. Move the text box so the side, top and bottom handles line up with the guides (Figure 4.6).

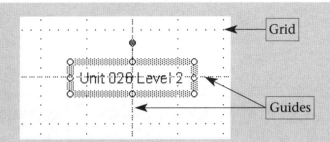

Figure 4.6 Using guides

6   Align the WordArt at the bottom of the page so it is in the centre and its top handles are resting on the grid line that is 2 cm below the zero marker.

7   Align the WordArt at the top of the page so it is in the centre and its bottom handles are resting on the grid line that is 2 cm above the zero marker.

8   Save the presentation.

Task 4.4   Change text box properties

Method

1   Insert a new blank slide.

2   Create a text box and key in the website address **www.e-quals.co.uk**. If it changes colour and an underscore appears, click on **Undo**. It means that it has been recognised as a link to a website.

3   With the cursor inside the text box, click on the **Line Style** button ≣ (Figure 4.7) and choose a line style and weight.

Figure 4.7 Drawing toolbar

4   Click on **Dash Style** and choose a style (Figure 4.7).

5   Click on the dropdown arrow beside **Fill Color** 🪣 ▾ and choose a colour from **More Fill colors**.

6   Click on the dropdown arrow beside **Line Color** 🖌 ▾ and choose a different colour in the same way.

7   Position the pointer over the green rotate handle and drag the mouse a little in any direction.

8   To rotate to a specific angle, choose **Text Box** from the **Format** menu. Notice you can change line styles and colour etc. from here also.

9 Click on the **Size** tab (Figure 4.8) and key in **25** in the **Rotation** box. Click **OK.**

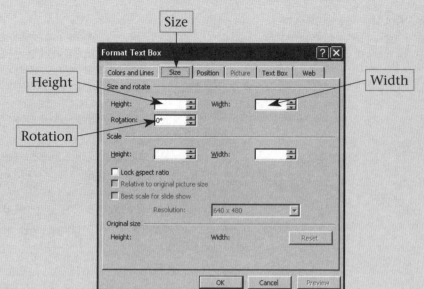

Figure 4.8 Format text box

10 Move the text box into the top left quarter of the slide.
11 Save the presentation.

Information: Text wrap and resize

The text box created in Task 4.2 automatically resized to fit the text as you keyed in. If you carried on typing, the text would eventually go off the slide. You can, however, insert a text box by dragging to create a rectangle of the required width. Any text keyed into this text box will **word wrap** onto the next line when it reaches the far side. Whilst the width of the text box will remain the same, it will grow downwards to accommodate more text as it is entered.

Task 4.5	Draw a text box

Method

1 Click on the **Text Box** tool and draw a text box in the bottom left quarter of the slide, roughly the same width and depth as the existing one.
2 Key in the following text. Allow the text to word wrap – do not press Enter.

Whilst the width of the text box will remain the same, it will grow downwards as more text is entered.

The reason why this happens is because **Word wrap** and **Resize** are default settings for a drawn text box. Check this now:

3 Select **Text Box** from the **Format** menu. (Ensure the text box is selected first.) Select the **Text Box** tab (Figure 4.9). Notice the settings. Click **Cancel**.

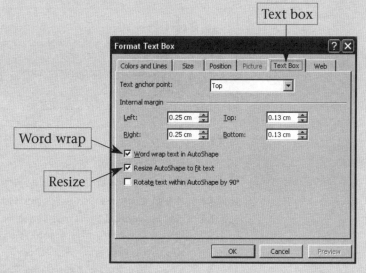

Figure 4.9 Word wrap and resize

4 Click on the **Text Box** tool ▣ and then click in the bottom right quarter of the slide.

5 Select **Text Box** from the **Format** menu and click on the **Text Box** tab (Figure 4.9). Notice that word wrap is no longer selected.

6 Click **Cancel** and key in the following to see what happens:
Text keyed into this type of text box will eventually go off the edge of the slide.

7 Save presentation.

Information review: Text boxes

Text can be created in two ways, both of which require the **Text Box** tool ▣ :

1 **Click where text is required and type**. Text does not word wrap.
2 **Drag and draw a text box**. Text will word wrap. The text box will grow downwards to accommodate text keyed in.

The text in these text boxes will not appear in the Outline pane.

Information: Tabs

Tab stops can be set across a text box, at points where you wish to line up text, so allowing you to set it up in columns.

Method

1   Insert a new blank slide.
2   Ensure the rule is displayed and draw a text box almost the full width of the slide.

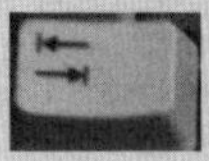

Figure 4.10 Tab key

3   Click on the ruler just below the 8 cm point this sets a tab stop.
4   Key in **Country** and press the **Tab** key.
5   Key in **Capital** and press **Enter** to start a new line.
6   Key in **Austria** and press the **Tab** key.
7   Key in **Vienna** and press **Enter** to start a new line.
8   Key in **Belgium** and press the **Tab** key.
9   Key in **Brussels** and press **Enter** to start a new line.
10   Repeat this process keying in the following

- **Denmark**   **Copenhagen**
- **France**   **Paris**
- **Germany**   **Berlin**
- **Greece**   **Ireland**

11   Save the presentation.

→ Practise your skills 4.1

1   Open a new presentation with a blank slide.
2   Insert WordArt, keying in the words **Colours of the Rainbow**.
3   Show the rulers and guides and line up the WordArt centrally on the slide.
4   Insert a new blank slide.
5   Insert a text box and key in **red**.
6   Insert another text box and key in **orange**.
7   Repeat for the following colours: **yellow**, **green**, **blue**, **indigo**, **violet**.
8   Change the fill colour of the red text box to red.
9   Repeat for each text box so that it displays the colour it describes. (**Hint**: Indigo is a dark navy blue).
10   Change the text colour of each text box to white. You can do this in one go, by choosing **Select All** from the **Edit** menu first.
11   Change the width of each box to **3 cm**.
12   Add a **1 pt** style line border around each text box.
13   Rotate the orange text box by **30°**.
14   Rotate the yellow text box by **60°**.
15   Rotate the green text box by **90°**.

16 Rotate the blue text box by **−60°**. (Using a minus figure rotates text in the other direction.)

17 Rotate the indigo text box by **−30°**.

18 Drag a guide up **4 cm** from the horizontal guide.

19 Drag a guide **4 cm** to the left of the vertical (upright) guide.

20 Drag a guide **4 cm** to the right of the vertical (upright) guide.

21 Align the red, green and violet boxes with the guides as shown in Figure 4.11 and arrange the others in between.

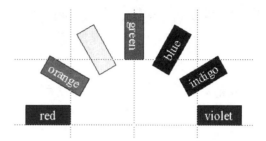

Figure 4.11 Align with guides

22 Drag and draw a text box in the bottom left section of the slide and key in the following:

The colours are arranged in this order, often remembered by their initial letters ROY G BIV

23 Insert another text in the bottom right corner of the slide and key in the following:

A rainbow starts with red on the outside and moves through the colours to violet on the inside.

24 Format these two text boxes to a height and width of **7 cm**.

25 Add a border with a long dash line style to both.

26 Drag another guide down **7 cm** from the middle.

27 Align the two text boxes with this guide.

28 Add your name, date and page number to the footer.

29 Insert a new blank slide and draw a text box almost across the width of the slide.

30 Set a tab at **7 cm** and **14 cm**.

31 Key in the following:

Dark Red	**Orange**	**Teal**
Red	**Tan**	**Aqua**
Pink Gold	**Sea**	**Green**
Salmon	**Peach**	**Lime green**

32 Proofread and check spelling.

33 Save as **Rainbow** into the **Skills Practice Level 2** folder and print as handouts, three to a page.

→ Check your knowledge

1 What might WordArt be used for?

2 There are two ways of creating text boxes. What are they?

3 What is the difference between them in the way that text behaves when keyed in?

4 Identify the following buttons on the Drawing toolbar.

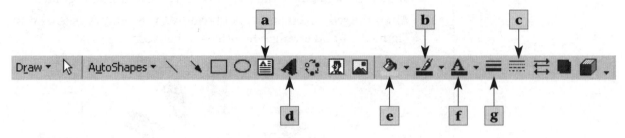

Figure 4.12 Drawing toolbar

Hint:

When you cannot remember what each button is for, position the pointer over each one and a description will appear.

Section 5

Text from other sources

You will learn to:

- Import text from a text file
- Copy and paste text from a text file
- Format text with bullets and indenting
- Copy and paste text from a web browser

Before carrying out the tasks in this unit you will need the following text files:

- Countries
- Colds and Flu
- Prevention and Treatment
- Car Security

Instructions for creating these files can be found in the Appendix or your tutor may supply them.

Whilst text is usually keyed directly into PowerPoint, it can also be imported from a text file or copied and pasted from other sources.

Hint:

An intranet is a series of web pages internal to an organisation and access is usually confined to its employees/users. Your college or employer probably has an intranet.

Information

Text can be imported into PowerPoint from a variety of sources – text files on your computer, from disk, CD, the Internet or an intranet using a web browser.

Task 5.1 — Import text from a text file

For this task you will need the text file **Countries** stored in a folder called **Text files**. (see Appendix or check with your tutor). This file contains a list of headings – the outline for a presentation. Make sure the text file is closed before importing it.

Method

1 Open a new presentation with a Title slide and key in the title **Worldwide Office Locations**.
2 Click on the **Outline** tab on the left of the slide window.
3 Select **Slides from Outline** from the **Insert** menu.
4 Select the folder **Text files** and click **Open** (Figure 5.1).

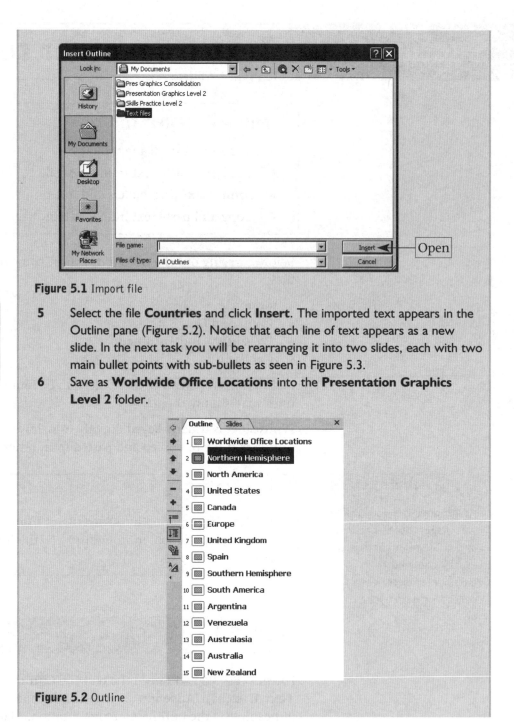

Figure 5.1 Import file

Remember:

Did you remember to close the text file before importing?

5   Select the file **Countries** and click **Insert**. The imported text appears in the Outline pane (Figure 5.2). Notice that each line of text appears as a new slide. In the next task you will be rearranging it into two slides, each with two main bullet points with sub-bullets as seen in Figure 5.3.

6   Save as **Worldwide Office Locations** into the **Presentation Graphics Level 2** folder.

Figure 5.2 Outline

Task 5.2   Promote and demote outline points

The **Promote** button ⬅ makes a point more important (see Figure 5.3).

The **Demote** button ➡ makes a point less important.

Bullets are useful for presenting facts in a list. Sometimes one bullet point will have a further list of sub-items which are less important than the main item, as seen in Figure 5.3.

Hint:

The **Tab** key can be used instead of **Demote** by placing the cursor in front of the text to be demoted.
Experiment with the

Promote ◀ button to see its effect. A bullet point will become a slide title and a sub-bullet will become a main bullet point. End up with the outline as it appears in Figure 5.3.
Promote and **Demote** are also used for indenting text without bullets. You might do this in order to make a paragraph stand out from the rest of the text.

Hint:

You can also use **Decrease Indent** ◀≡ and **Increase**

Indent ≡▶ instead of **Promote** and **Demote**.

Method

1 In the Outline pane, highlight from **North America** down to **Spain**. These items will form bullet points on the Northern Hemisphere slide.
2 Click on **Demote** ▶.
3 Highlight from **South America** down to **New Zealand**. These items will form bullet points on the Southern Hemisphere slide.
4 Click on **Demote** ▶.
5 Highlight **United States** and **Canada**. These items will become sub-bullets.
6 Click on **Demote** ▶.
7 Highlight **United Kingdom** and **Spain** and click on **Demote** ▶.
8 Highlight **Argentina** and **Venezuela** and click on **Demote** ▶.
9 Highlight **Australia** and **New Zealand** and click on **Demote** ▶.
10 Save the presentation. The Outline pane should resemble Figure 5.3. You will print in the next task.

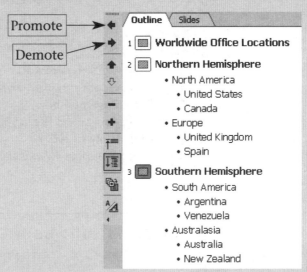

Figure 5.3 Outline with bullets

Information

The Outline pane can be used to key in the text of a presentation. Each time a new slide is required press **Enter,** or **Promote/Demote** as necessary.

Task 5.3   Add a header or footer to an Outline printout

You have already added footers to the bottom of slides but you can also include headers as well as footers on other printouts such as handouts, outlines and notes. (Notes are featured in a later section.)

Method

1   Select **Header and Footer** from the **View** menu.
2   Click on the **Notes and Handouts** tab (Figure 5.4). This is very similar to the Slide Header and Footer window with the added ability to include a header.

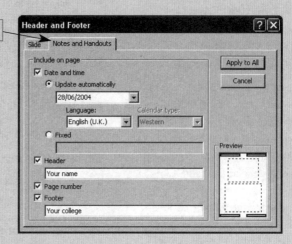

Notes and Handouts

Figure 5.4 Header and Footer – Notes and Handouts

3   Select **Update automatically** for the date.
4   Select **Header** and key in your name.
5   Select **Page number**.
6   Select **Footer** and key in your college name, or company name if applicable.
7   Click **Apply to All**.
8   Print an **Outline** view, save and close the presentation.

Information: Copy and paste text from another source

Copy and paste is a feature you should already be familiar with. It enables you to copy information from one place in a file/document/presentation to another. It can also be used to copy from another application or a web browser. If you are using text (or indeed graphics) from a source such as the Internet, you must make sure it is copyright-free or that you have permission to use it, otherwise you may be breaking copyright law. Copyright means that the creator or owner has the right to control who can make copies and how their work can be used. Some sites may allow free usage when their material is used for non-commercial purposes and/or an acknowledgement is given to its source.

Task 5.4 — Copy and paste text from a text file

Method

1 Open a new presentation with a Title slide and key in the title **Continents**.
2 Save the presentation as **Continents** into the **Presentation Graphics Level 2** folder.
3 Insert a new **Bulleted List** slide.
4 Open Word and the text file **Countries** – you can switch between the two programs and the files by clicking on whichever is required on the taskbar at the bottom of the screen (Figure 5.5). Try this now.

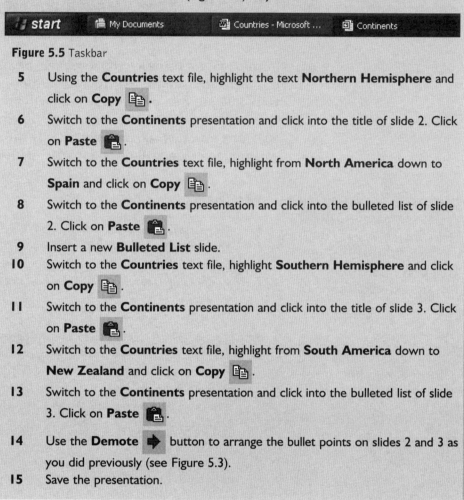

Figure 5.5 Taskbar

5 Using the **Countries** text file, highlight the text **Northern Hemisphere** and click on **Copy** .
6 Switch to the **Continents** presentation and click into the title of slide 2. Click on **Paste** .
7 Switch to the **Countries** text file, highlight from **North America** down to **Spain** and click on **Copy** .
8 Switch to the **Continents** presentation and click into the bulleted list of slide 2. Click on **Paste** .
9 Insert a new **Bulleted List** slide.
10 Switch to the **Countries** text file, highlight **Southern Hemisphere** and click on **Copy** .
11 Switch to the **Continents** presentation and click into the title of slide 3. Click on **Paste** .
12 Switch to the **Countries** text file, highlight from **South America** down to **New Zealand** and click on **Copy** .
13 Switch to the **Continents** presentation and click into the bulleted list of slide 3. Click on **Paste** .
14 Use the **Demote** button to arrange the bullet points on slides 2 and 3 as you did previously (see Figure 5.3).
15 Save the presentation.

Task 5.5 — Remove and add bullet points

Bullet points are not always required and they are very easy to remove or to add to a slide.

Method

1 Using the **Northern Hemisphere** slide of the same presentation, highlight all of the bulleted text and click on the **Bullets** button to remove them.

2	Repeat this process on the **Southern Hemisphere** slide.
3	With the same text highlighted, click on the **Bullets** button to add them.
4	Repeat on the other slide.
5	Add a footer to show your name on each slide and a header to show your name on an Outline printout.
6	Check the presentation and view it.
7	Print an Outline.
8	Save the presentation and close.

Task 5.6 — Copy and paste text from a web browser

Instructions for using a web browser are beyond the scope of this book and it is therefore assumed that you will already be able to do this. For this task you could use your own college intranet, if they have one, or their website. Copying text from a web browser is no different to copying it from anywhere else. Just take care not to copy white text onto a white background or you will not see it when pasted!

Remember:

There is a difference between a **Title** slide and a **Title Only** slide. Make sure you select the right one.

Remember:

A hyperlink is text or an image that links to another location.

Method

1	Open a new presentation and using a **Title** slide, key in the title **Words from the web**.
2	Save it as **Words from the web** into the **Presentation Graphics Level 2** folder.
3	Insert a new **Title Only** slide and key in the heading **Text pasted into slide view**.
4	Using the **Text Box** tool 🔲, draw a text box across the slide.
5	Load your web browser and visit the page of your choice.
6	Highlight two sentences of text or three or four short bulleted items that do not include a hyperlink and choose **Copy** from the **Edit** menu. (You must position the cursor very close to the first letter of the text to be highlighted.)
7	Switch to the presentation **Words from the web** and with the cursor in the text box, click on **Paste** 📋. You may need to adjust the layout depending on the text chosen.
8	Save the presentation, view it and close.

Information: Copying and pasting into Outline view

1 Insert a new **Title Only** slide and using the **Outline** pane, key in the heading **Text pasted into outline view**.

2 Press **Enter** – notice how PowerPoint starts a new slide. As this is not what is required, click on **Demote** ➡️.

3 Load your browser and locate a web page with three or four short bullet points.

4 Highlight and copy them using **Copy** from the **Edit** menu. ➡️

5 Switch back to the PowerPoint and click on **Paste**. You may need to adjust the layout and formatting depending on the text selected.

6 Add your name in the footer.

7 View the presentation.

8 Save the presentation, print as **handouts, three to a page**, and an **Outline** view. Then close.

Information: Which is the best method for bringing text into a presentation?

It depends what you need to do. Importing text using **Slides from Outline** on the **Insert** menu works well for straightforward lists. **Copying and pasting** into Outline view can be unpredictable – it is easier to paste text into a title or text box on the slide itself, a section at a time, and then adjust the text to suit.

Information: Exporting from Word

This process is not required for e-Quals but you may like to try it. It is possible to export text **to** PowerPoint **from** Word. Open Word and the **Countries** text file. Choose **File** menu – **Send to** and select **Microsoft PowerPoint**. A PowerPoint presentation should open with the text in place, as in Figure 5.2.

Hint:

Exporting from Word: If you are familiar with Word styles and heading styles used for each title, bullet and sub-bullet, the presentation would appear as in Figure 5.3.

→ Practise your skills 5.1

This task requires the use of the text file **Colds and Flu** in the folder **Text files** (see Appendix or check with your tutor). Make sure the text file is not open.

1 Open a new presentation with a **Title** slide and using **Outline** view, key in the title **Winter Ailments**.

2 Select **Slides from Outline** from the **Insert** menu.

3 Select **Colds and Flu** from the **Text files** folder. You should end up with 17 slides. If you have any blank slides, delete them.

4 Using **Demote** and **Promote** as necessary, arrange the text as seen in Figure 5.6. Notice that slide 2 has bullets and sub-bullets, whilst slide 3 has a further level of sub-bullets.

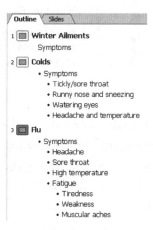

Figure 5.6 Imported text

→ Practise your skills 5.2

For this task you will require the text file **Prevention and Treatment** in the folder **Text files** (see Appendix or check with your tutor).

1 Open the text file **Prevention and Treatment** and the presentation **Winter Ailments**.

2 Click on the last slide and insert a new **Title Only** slide in the presentation. Key in the title **Prevention**.

3 Use the Text Box tool to draw a text box across the slide below the heading.

4 Switch to the text file, highlight and copy the Prevention paragraph (not the heading).

5 Switch to the presentation and paste the text into the text box.

6 Display the ruler, grid and guides and line up the text box so it is centred horizontally and vertically on the guides.

7 Insert another new **Title Only** slide and key in the heading **Treatment**.

8 Use the Text Box tool to draw a text box across the slide below the heading.

9 Switch to the text file, highlight and copy the remaining text, including the headings.

10 Switch to the presentation and paste the text into the text box.

11 Indent the paragraphs only below each of the **Treatment for ...** headings.

12 Line up the top of the text box with the 4 cm point on the ruler on the left guide, ensuring the middle handle is still on the vertical (upright) guide (Figure 5.7).

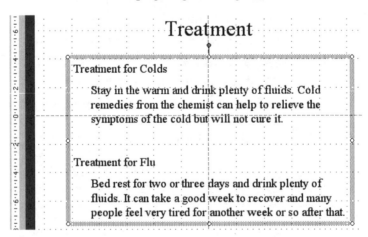

Figure 5.7 Lining up with guides

13 Insert another **Title Only** slide with the heading **Did you know?**

14 Create a text box across the slide below the heading.

15 Load your web browser and search for facts on flu and colds. Copy a small amount of text (three or four sentences) and paste into the slide. Amend the text if necessary.

16 Line up the text box centrally on the slide.

17 Change the **subtitle** on slide 1 to read **Symptoms and Treatment**.

18 Save the presentation as **Winter Ailments Version 2**.

19 Change the layout of slide 2 to **Title, Text and Clip Art** and find a suitable clip art image.

20 Change the layout of slide 3 to **Title, Clip Art and Text** and find a suitable clip art image.

21 View the presentation.

22 Save and print as handouts, six to a page. Close.

→ Check your knowledge

1 What are these buttons called and what do they do?

(a) ◄   (b) ►

2 When might you use bullet points?

3 When might you indent text?

4 List possible sources of text that can be inserted into a presentation.

5 Why is the issue of copyright important when copying information from the Internet?

Consolidation 2

You will need the text file **Car Security** for this task in the folder **Text files** (see Appendix or check with your tutor). As you will be importing the text, make sure the text file is not open.

A new template is required for Smarts Driving School that they can use for all their presentations. Your task is to set one up and then to create a presentation using a copy of it.

1 Open a new blank presentation.

2 Format the background with a **two-colour gradient** effect using two shades of blue (use a pale blue and a mid blue) with a shading style **From corner**. Apply to all slides.

3 On the Master slide change the title style and the text style to one of your choice. Choose a text colour for all text including the footer items.

4 Insert a clip art image of a car and place in the top left corner.

5 Format the picture to a height of **2 cm,** locking aspect ratio to keep it in proportion.

6 Insert a Title Master.

7 On the Title Master resize the image to **4 cm** high locking aspect ratio.

8 Move the image to the middle of the slide above the title and using the ruler and guide, ensure it is in the centre.

9 Embolden the title and subtitle.

10 Change to Normal view and key in the title **Smarts Driving School**.

11 Insert a footer to show the date, the slide number and your name in the slide footer (choose a date style). The footer is not required on the Title slide.

12 Insert a header on Notes and Handouts to display your name with the date and page number.

13 Save the file as a design template with the name **Smarts Driving School**.

14 Close the template file.

15 Open a copy of the new template and show it to your tutor.

16 Using **Slides from Outline** on the **Insert** menu, import the text file **Car Security** from the **Text files** folder.

17 Using Demote/Promote, organise the slides as shown in Figure 5.8.

18 On the first slide add the subtitle **Keep it safe**.

19 Change the layout of the second slide to **Text and Clip Art**, and insert suitable clip art.

20 Save the presentation as **Car Security** into the **Presentation Graphics Consolidation** folder. Print an Outline.

21 Insert a new **Title Only** slide and key in the title **And finally** .

22 Draw a text box across the slide below the heading.

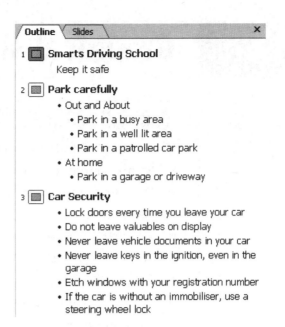

Figure 5.8 Outline view

23 Load your web browser and look for a short piece of information about **car security** on which to finish the presentation.

24 Copy and paste it into the last slide. Edit it as necessary to suit.

25 Format it to match the other slides. (Drawn text boxes do not take on the formatting of the Master slides.)

26 Using the ruler and guides, centre the text frame.

27 Change the layout of slide 2 (Park carefully) to **Title, Text and Clip Art**. Insert a suitable image.

28 Move slide 3 (Car Security) to become slide 2.

29 Insert a new blank slide as the last slide and insert WordArt of your choice to read **Don't be a victim**.

30 Resize the WordArt to a height of **5** and a width of **15**.

31 Position it in the centre of the slide and then rotate it by **20°** so it is sloping upwards from left to right.

32 Check the presentation carefully and view it.

33 Save as **Car Security Version 2** and print as handouts, six to a page.

You will learn to:

- Create graphical shapes using AutoShapes
- Format graphical shapes
- Draw lines and connectors
- Create callouts
- Add text to shapes
- Work with layers
- Group objects together
- Copy and paste to another slide
- Flip and rotate objects

This section covers the creation of graphical shapes and how to manipulate them. Shapes can be used on their own or combined with other graphical features such as clip art and text to illustrate slides.

Information: Predefined shapes

PowerPoint has a variety of pre-defined shapes which can be used on their own or in combination with other shapes, images and text. The Drawing toolbar is used to create these shapes and you will already be familiar with some of its features. If the Drawing toolbar is not visible at the bottom of the window, select **Toolbars** from the **View** menu and then **Drawing**.

Task 6.1   Using shapes and AutoShapes

Method

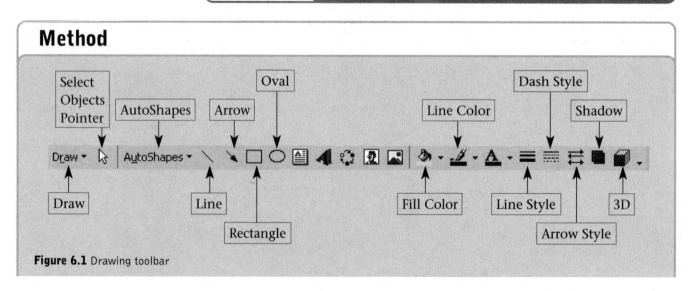

Figure 6.1 Drawing toolbar

1 Open a new presentation with a Title slide and key in the heading **Working with graphical shapes**.

2 Save it as **Graphical shapes** in the **Presentation Graphics Level 2** folder.

3 Insert a new **Title Only** slide and key in the heading **Shapes**.

4 Try each of the following tools in turn. Select the tool and press and drag to draw the shape on the slide:

   Rectangle   Oval   Line   Arrow

   Some lines/edges may appear jagged onscreen.

5 Try making the following changes – experiment with different shapes. Select a shape first with the **Select Objects Pointer** .

   - **Resize a shape** – select and drag a handle.
   - **Move a shape** – select and drag the shape (avoid handles).
   - **Change the colour** – select and click on the **Fill Color** dropdown arrow and select from **More Fill Colors**. **No Fill** is transparent.
   - **Change the line style** – select and click on **Line Style** .
   - **Change to a dash style** – select and click on **Dash Style**.
   - **Change line colour** – select and click on the **Line Color** dropdown arrow and select from **More Line Colors**.
   - **Apply a Shadow or 3-D effect** – select a shape and click on **Shadow** or **3-D** . (You will lose line colour and line styles applied.)
   - **Change arrow style** – select or draw a line and click on **Arrow Style** .
   - **Rotate a shape** – drag the green rotate handle to left or right.
   - **Delete a shape** – select a shape and press **Delete** on the keyboard.

6 Delete all shapes.

7 Click on **AutoShapes** – a menu appears (Figure 6.2). Click on **Basic Shapes**. As you move the pointer over the shapes, a tip appears showing their names. Select any of the shapes and press and drag on the slide to draw it. Use other shapes in the Basic Shapes category.

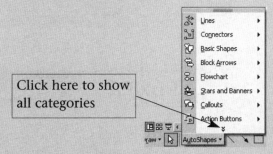

Figure 6.2 AutoShapes

8 Some shapes have an **adjustment handle** (a yellow diamond) which can be used to change a feature of the shape. Use the **Sun** tool (Figure 6.2) to draw a shape and try dragging the adjustment handle in different directions.

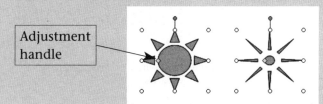

Figure 6.3 Sun shape with adjustment handle

Hint:

To draw a perfect circle or a perfect square, hold the Shift key when using the Rectangle or Oval tools.

Hint:

Line style and Dash style can be used on lines or shapes.

Hint:

You can also rotate shapes by using the **Format** menu – **AutoShape** – **Size** tab and keying in an angle of rotation as you did with text boxes in Section 4.

Hint:

There are several different categories of AutoShapes, each with a variety of options.

9   Experiment with other shapes in the **Basic Shapes** category and their adjustment handles.

10   Delete shapes as necessary to create space.

11   Experiment with **Fill Color** (including **No Fill**), **Line Color** and **Line Style**.

12   Experiment with shapes from the **Block Arrows**, **Flowchart** and **Stars and Banners** categories.

13   Save.

Task 6.2   Resize a shape to a specific size

Method

1   Click on **AutoShapes** and select **Basic Shapes**. Select the **Regular Pentagon** tool and draw a shape.

2   With the shape selected, select **AutoShape** from the **Format** menu (Figure 6.4).

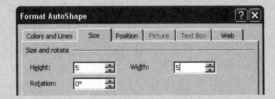

Figure 6.4 Format AutoShape

3   Click on the **Size** tab and enter a height of **5 cm** and a width of **5 cm**. Click **OK**.

4   Draw a **Trapezoid** shape and format it to a height and width of **7 cm**.

5   Position the trapezoid directly on top of the pentagon – you will need them in the next task.

6   Save.

Task 6.3   Set semitransparent fill

No Fill means that an object is transparent – you can see through it. **Semitransparent** means you can partially see through it. This can be achieved not only with shapes, but also with text boxes.

Drag the slider to the right to increase transparency. The result is shown in the Color box above.

Figure 6.5 Format – Transparent fill

Method

I   Select the trapezoid created in the last task.

2   Select **AutoShape** from the **Format** menu and change transparency to 50% (Figure 6.5) and click **OK**. You should be able to see the pentagon beneath it through the semitransparent colour.

3   Create a **text box** and key in your name.

4   Fill the text box with a colour of your choice and position it on top of the trapezoid.

5   Select **Text Box** from the **Format** menu and change transparency to 60%. You should be able to see through the shapes.

6   Save.

Information: Drawing lines

You have already used the **Line** and **Arrow** tools on the Drawing toolbar. There is also an AutoShapes **Lines** category as well as **Connectors**, which are used to join objects together.

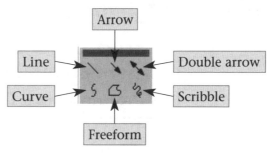

Figure 6.6 AutoShapes – Lines

Task 6.4   Drawing lines and connectors

Hint:

The **Line Style**, **Dash Style** and **Arrow Style** options can be used with any of the **Lines** category tools.

Method

I   Insert a new **Title Only** slide and key in the heading **Working with lines**.

2   Click on **AutoShapes** and select **Lines** (Figure 6.6).

3   **Line** and **Arrow** are the same as those on the Drawing toolbar. Click on **Double arrow** and drag on the slide to draw.

4   Try each of the following line types:

   Curve   Drag and click where you want a curve. Double-click to end.

   Freeform   Combine freehand and straight lines. Drag to draw freehand shapes, click to add straight lines. Double-click to end.

   Scribble   Drag and draw as if using a pen. Pause to end.

5   Insert a new **Title Only** slide and key in the heading **Working with Connectors**.

6   Select **Connectors** from **AutoShapes** and choose any of the tools. If the Connectors category does not appear, click on the down arrow at the bottom of the list – see Figure 6.2.

   Connectors are of three styles – **straight** lines, **jointed** lines or **curves**, with or without arrowheads.

7	Drag on the slide to draw a connector.
8	Click on the **Dash Style** button on the **Drawing** toolbar and select a style.
9	Click on the **Line Color** arrow and choose a colour from **More Line Colors**.
10	Click on the **Line Style** button on the **Drawing** toolbar and select a style.
11	Drag a handle to change the size of the line.
12	Drag on the **adjustor handle** to modify the line.
13	Experiment with other connectors.
14	Draw two rectangle shapes.
15	Select a connector and position over one of the shapes. Connector points appear as blue squares. Drag to the second shape to join them together. The shapes are now attached but can you move each of them separately? Try it.
16	To separate the connector, drag on the connector line and move it.
17	To reattach a connector, drag the end of the connector over the shape and reposition.
18	Experiment with shapes and connectors to familiarise yourself with the way they work.
19	Save.

Information: Callouts

Callouts enable you to label diagrams or other images.

Task 6.5 — Using callouts

Method

1	Insert a new **Title Only** slide and key in the heading **Working with callouts**.
2	Select **Callouts** from **AutoShapes** and choose a callout style.
3	Press and drag on the slide to create a shape and key in your name. Resize the callout if necessary or the text size.
4	With the shape selected, click on the **Fill Color** icon and **No Fill** (for a transparent effect). Experiment with Callouts before moving on.
5	Using **Basic Shapes** from **AutoShapes** draw a **Heart**. Change the **Fill Color** to red.
6	Use a callout to label the shape **Heart**. Change the **Fill Color** to **No Fill**.
7	Save.

Information: Adding text to shapes

Text can be added to any shape (except lines). Simply select a shape and start to key in text. If necessary word wrap can be applied to the shape.

Task 6.6   Adding text to shapes

Method

1. Insert a new **Title Only** slide and key in the heading **Adding text to shapes**.
2. Using **Basic Shapes** from **AutoShapes** draw a **Parallelogram**.
3. Ensure the shape is selected and key in its name – **Parallelogram**.
4. Repeat with several other shapes of your choice – resize as necessary to ensure text fits.
5. Word wrap can be applied to shapes when required. Draw a **Rectangle** and format it to a height or width of **4 cm** and key in **Adding text to shapes**. Select **Autoshapes** from the **Format** menu and on the **Text Box** tab, select **Word wrap text in AutoShape**. Click **OK**.
6. Save.

Information: Working with layers

When you have several objects overlapping or directly on top of one another you have **layers**. These can be arranged by reordering the layers – bringing one object to the front of the pile or sending another to the back of the pile. Each layer can be handled and formatted separately.

Task 6.7   Working with layers

Method

1. Insert a new **Title Only** slide and key in the heading **Working with layers**.
2. Draw a **Rectangle** shape and using **AutoShape** on the **Format** menu, resize the shape to **10 cm** by **10 cm**.
3. Draw a **Rounded rectangle** shape and resize the shape to **7 cm** by **7 cm**. Change its colour.
4. Insert an image from **ClipArt** and using **Picture** on the **Format** menu, change the height of the image to **5 cm** with locked aspect ratio.
5. Insert a **text box** and key in a title for your image.
6. Arrange the objects as shown in Figure 6.7.

Figure 6.7 Layers

Figure 6.8 Order layers

7. Select the **ClipArt** picture and click on **Draw** on the **Drawing** toolbar (Figure 6.8). Click on **Order** and **Send to Back** from the side menu. The picture disappears although the handles remain.

8 Select the **Rounded rectangle** and click on **Draw** on the **Drawing** toolbar. Click on **Order** and **Send Backward** from the side menu.

Bring to Front	Bring the selected object to the front
Send to Back	Send the selected object to the back
Bring Forward	Bring the selected object forward by one layer
Send Backward	Send the selected object back by one layer

9 Use these options to bring the layers back to their original position.

10 Save.

Hint:

If you 'lose' a layer when reordering, you can always drag each object to one side and rearrange them!

Information: Grouping objects

When you are working with several objects it is useful to **group** them together as they can then be moved, resized or copied as one object. This is much easier than dealing with lots of single objects. If you need to change one object within a group, then you can easily **ungroup** them.

Task 6.8 | Group and ungroup objects

There are two ways of selecting a group of objects.

Method 1

1 Using the same slide created in the last task, click on the **Select Objects** pointer.

2 Position it at position **1** as in seen in Figure 6.9 and drag across and down to position **2** – as you do this, a dotted line rectangle appears.

3 Release the mouse and handles appear on all objects enclosed within that space (Figure 6.10).

Figure 6.9 Select objects   **Figure 6.10** Selected objects

4 Click on a blank area of the slide to deselect them.

Method 2

1 Click on one object, hold down the **Shift** key and click on each of the other three objects in turn. Each should appear selected.

2 Click on **Draw** on the **Drawing** toolbar and select **Group**. One set of handles should appear on the grouped object.

3 Move the object by dragging.

4 Copy the object by clicking on **Copy** 📋 and then **Paste** 📋 on the **Standard** toolbar. Position the objects side by side.

5 Drag a corner handle of the right-hand grouped object to make it smaller, holding down the **Shift** key to lock aspect ratio. Notice that the text box is resized but the text is not.

6 Click on **Undo** ↺.

7 Highlight the text label of the same grouped object and change its size to **10**.

8 Resize the object again to make it smaller, still holding down the **Shift** key.

9 Resize the object to **7 cm** by **7 cm** using **Object** from the **Format** menu.

10 To **ungroup** the object, select it and click on **Draw** on the **Drawing toolbar** and then **Ungroup**.

11 Click on a blank area of the slide to deselect the objects.

12 Reduce the size of the clip art image, holding the **Shift** key to keep it in proportion. Adjust its position as necessary.

13 With any of the objects in that same 'group' selected, click on **Draw** and then **Regroup**.

14 Save.

Remember:

Lock aspect ratio ensures the image remains in proportion and does not become distorted.

Hint:

As the object was already copied, it will still be held in the **Clipboard** – an area of Windows memory – until you are ready to paste it.

Task 6.9 — Copy and paste objects to other slides

You are already familiar with copy and paste. To copy an object to another slide, copy it, move to the required slide and paste.

Method

1 Select the smaller of the two grouped objects and **Copy** it.

2 Move to the first slide and delete the subtitle placeholder.

3 Click on **Paste** to paste the grouped object and position it below the title – resizing if necessary.

4 Move back to the last slide, insert a new **Title Only** slide and key in the heading **Copy and paste**.

5 Click on **Paste** to paste the grouped object onto this slide.

6 Save.

Information: Flip and rotate

Flipping means to turn an object over. **Flip Horizontal** means the object will face the opposite direction (mirrored). **Flip Vertical** will turn the object upside down. This is sometimes known as **inverting** an object. There is also a further method of rotating objects.

Task 6.10 — Flip and rotate

Method

1. Insert a new **Title Only** slide and key in the heading **Flipping and Rotating**.
2. Insert a **Lightning Bolt** from **AutoShapes – Basic Shapes** category and a **Chevron** from **Block Arrows**.
3. Select the **Chevron** shape and click on **Draw** and then **Rotate or Flip**. Click on **Flip Horizontal**.
4. Select the **Lightning Bolt** shape and click on **Draw** and then **Rotate or Flip**. Click on **Flip Vertical**.
5. With the same shape selected, click on **Draw** and then **Rotate or Flip**. Click on **Rotate Right**.
6. Experiment with these options.
7. Save.

Task 6.11 — Flip and rotate clip art

Select the clip art object now and try to flip it. You may find you cannot do this with some clip art. In this case you would need to convert it to a drawing object first by ungrouping.

Method

1. Select the clip art image and click on **Draw** and then **Ungroup**. A message appears asking if you wish to convert the image. Click on **Yes**.
2. Click on **Draw** and **Ungroup** again. The clip art image breaks down into a number of separate objects.
3. Click on **Draw – Group**. The image now becomes one object again.
4. Select the clip art image and click on **Draw** and then **Rotate or Flip**.
5. Try this out with another clip art image.
6. Add your name, date and slide number to the slides.
7. Print the presentation as handouts, six to a page.

→ Practise your skills 6.1

Create a new presentation for Robin Frames, a picture framing business that is putting together a presentation for new staff.

1 Start a new presentation.

2 Switch to the Master slide and create a background of two pale colours shading from the title.

3 Change the font for the entire master to one of your choice (make sure it is easy to read).

4 Change the bullet style for the first and second level bullets so they are the same.

5 Add your name and the date to the slide footer.

6 Switch to the Title slide and key in the title **Robin Frames** with a subtitle of **Staff Procedures**.

7 Insert a clip art image searching on the word **robin** (or **bird**) for a logo, resizing it to a height of **2 cm** and locking aspect ratio to keep it in proportion.

8 Create a text box and key in **Robin Frames** in your chosen font with a text size of **10**. Colour the text.

9 Group the image and the text box and position the grouped logo in the top right corner of the slide.

10 Copy the logo and place the copy in the top left corner.

11 Flip the copy horizontally. (Will you need to ungroup the logo and also the image first?)

12 Save the presentation as **Robin Frames** into the **Skills Practice Level 2** folder.

13 Insert a new **Title, Text and Clip Art** slide and key in a heading **Products**.

14 Key the following, indenting where shown:
- Picture framing
    - Standard size
    - Custom size
    - Special order
- Prints
- Mounts
- Accessories

15 Insert a suitable clip art image.

16 Insert a new blank slide and create the flowchart shown in Figure 6.11 to show the procedure for framing a picture.

Firstly, draw shapes from the **Flowchart** category of AutoShapes and arrange them using guides. (You could draw one of each shape and then copy and paste.)

Use two different fill colours for the shapes.

Use text size **18** for the shape labels.

Use **Straight Line Connectors** with arrowheads to join the shapes where indicated.

Use text boxes for the **yes** and **no** labels.

Use WordArt for the **Flowchart** heading in the top left corner.

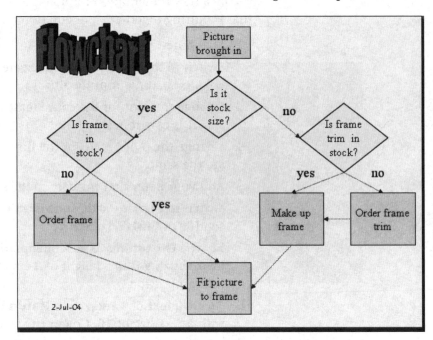

Figure 6.11 Flowchart

17 Insert a new **Title Only** slide and key in a heading **Frame Options**.

18 Draw a rectangle shape and resize it to **8 cm × 6 cm** and fill it with a dark colour

19 Draw a second rectangle of **7 cm × 5 cm** and fill it with a pale colour.

20 Position the smaller rectangle on top of the larger one to create a 'picture frame' (Figure 6.12).

21 **Group** the two shapes together and **copy** and **paste** them. Position one group on the left and one on the right.

22 **Rotate** the right-hand group to the left.

23 Insert a clip art image of a flower and resize it to fit within the left-hand frame.

Figure 6.12 Picture frame

24 **Copy** and **paste** the image and paste it **twice** into the right-hand frame. Resize if necessary.

➡

25 Create a text box and key in **PORTRAIT**. Use a pale colour and set the transparency to 60%.

26 Rotate the text box so that it slopes upwards from left to right at an angle of **45°** (−45°) and place it across the image on the left.

27 Create a similar text box and key in **LANDSCAPE** using a pale colour and set the transparency to 60%.

28 Rotate the text box so that it slopes upwards from left to right and place it across the images on the right.

29 Use the **Scribble line** tool to draw the 'string' at the top of the pictures.

30 Group the objects making up the picture frame on the left together and repeat for those on the right.

31 Insert a new **Title Only** slide and key in the heading **Office Staff**.

32 Draw a **Rectangle 2 cm × 5 cm** 'desk' with a pale **fill colour** and a **Dash style** border.

33 Copy and paste it **five** times. Arrange the shapes using guides as shown in Figure 6.13, and **rotate** where necessary. Label the desks.

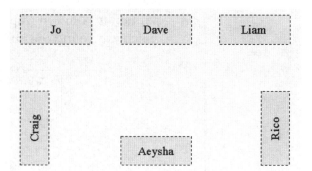

Figure 6.13 Staff

34 Insert a blank slide. Copy and paste the logo from the top right corner of slide 1 and paste it into the middle of the last slide.

35 Check the presentation and save it.

36 Print as handouts, six to a page.

37 Move slide 4 – Frame Options – to become slide 3.

38 Print slides 3 and 4 as handouts, two to a page.

39 Save and close

→ Practise your skills 6.2

1 Open the **Robin Frames** presentation from the **Skills Practice Level 2** folder.

2 Save it as **Robin Frames Version 2**.

3 Move to the last slide and **ungroup** the logo.

4 Increase the size of the clip art image to a height of **5 cm** retaining aspect ratio to keep it in proportion.

5 Increase the text size to **24** and adjust the text box size to ensure it fits onto one line.

6 Position the image in the centre of the slide using the guides, with the text below.

7 Draw a **Pentagon** shape and resize it to a height of **8 cm** and a width of **9 cm**.

8 Change its fill colour to one of your choice and position it centrally on the slide on top of the image and text.

9 Reorder the layers so the pentagon shape is sent to the back.

10 Insert a **Rounded Rectangular Callout** and change the fill colour to **white**. Key in the text as shown in Figure 6.14 and position it as shown (flip the callout if necessary, depending on which way round the bird is facing).

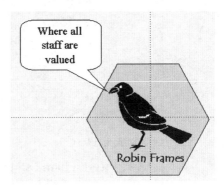

Figure 6.14 Callout

11 Group all four objects together.

12 Move to the **Flowchart** slide and change the linestyle of all the connectors to the **square dot** style.

13 Move to the last slide and insert a new **Title and 2-Column Text** slide – enter text as shown in Figure 6.15.

Figure 6.15 Staff slide

14 Insert a **Title and Text** slide and key in a heading **High Street Office Staff**. Key in the following, indenting the names after the first.

- **Craig MacDonald – Office Manager**
  - **Jo Drinkwater**
  - **Dave Roebuck**
  - **Liam Polanski**
  - **Aeysha Rosenberg**
  - **Rico Sanchez**

15 Copy the large grouped logo from slide 6 and paste it onto the **High Street Office Staff** slide and position it in the available space.

16 Change the order of the slides to the following:

Robin Frames Staff procedures

Shop Staff

High Street Office Staff

Office Staff

Products

Frame Options

Flowchart

Large logo

17 Check, save and print as handouts, nine to a page.

18 View the presentation.

→ Check your knowledge

1 How can you draw a perfect square or circle?

2 If you are required to draw a shape called Vertical Scroll, where would you find it and how would you know what it was?

3 What are the benefits of using layers?

4 Why is it useful to be able to group and ungroup objects?

5 What must you do to a clip art image in order to rotate or flip it?

Section 7 — Graphical images

You will learn to:

- Insert photographic images
- Crop and resize images
- Save images from an intranet/the Internet
- Copy and paste images from an intranet/the Internet
- Specify position of objects on a slide
- Use images for slide backgrounds

You have previously used clip art and graphical shapes and in this section you will insert photographic images to illustrate slides and use as backgrounds. You will also learn about other types of image that can be used. Access to sample photographic images and an intranet or the Internet, using a web browser such as Internet Explorer, will be needed.

Information: Photographic images

Photographic images can come from a variety of sources. You might create your own using a digital camera or scanner, purchase image libraries on CD-ROM or find them in PowerPoint Clip Organizer. You might also find them on the Internet or your college intranet. If you are using images for commercial purposes they should be copyright free unless you have permission to use them. If you use a 'free' site, it is likely to display conditions for using its images.

Task 7.1 — Insert a photographic image and resize

Hint:

Insert images from any location using this method.

This method of inserting a graphic image is the same whatever type of graphic file you want to insert and wherever it is stored. You will need access to photographic images stored on a network, hard disk, floppy disk, or CD-ROM. For practice purposes the subject is not important.

Method

1   Start a new blank presentation with a **Title** slide – heading **Images**.
2   Insert a new **Title Only** slide and key in the heading **Photographic image**.
3   Click on **Insert** menu and choose **Picture**. From the side menu select **From File**.
4   You now need to locate the image you require, see Figure 7.1. Do one of the following:

If it is in My Documents, click on **My Documents** in the left sidebar and then locate the required folder. Locate the picture you require and click on **Insert**.

If it is on floppy disk or CD, click on the dropdown arrow by the **Look in** box and locate the required drive. (Your Look in: list will be different to the example.) In Figure 7.1 the image is on a CD in E: drive. Locate the picture you require and click on **Insert**.

Figure 7.1 Insert Picture

> **Note:** If the picture is very large and you cannot see the handles to resize it, click on it to ensure it is selected and choose **Picture** from the **Format** menu. Click on the **Size** tab and key in a height of **10 cm**, **lock aspect ratio** to keep it in proportion and click **OK**. It should now be a manageable size.

5   Move the picture by dragging on the picture itself (avoid the handles).
6   Resize the picture by dragging on a corner handle. This will keep the picture in proportion whereas using a side handle will distort it.
7   Resize by using **Picture** from the **Format** menu. Click on the **Size** tab and key in a height of **5 cm**, locking aspect ratio to keep it in proportion, and click **OK**.

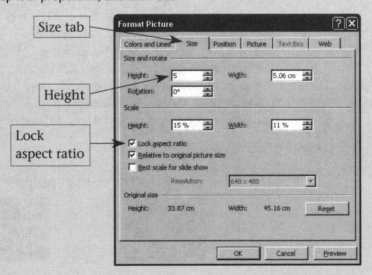

Figure 7.2 Format Picture

8   Insert another picture and resize it to a width of **5 cm**, locking aspect ratio.
9   Position the pictures in the top half of the slide, one on the left and one on the right.
10   Copy and paste each picture and place it below the original.
11   Save using the filename **Images** into the **Presentation Graphics Level 2** folder.

Information: Cropping images

Cropping is a process that allows you to cut off the sides of an image to remove unwanted areas. This is not permanent however, as you can 'uncrop' it to return it back to its original form. You can also do this with clip art images.

Task 7.2 — Crop an image and add a border

Method

1   Select the image in the bottom left corner. The **Picture** toolbar (Figure 7.3) should appear. If it does not, select **Toolbars** from the **View** menu and then **Picture**.

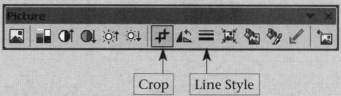

Figure 7.3 Picture toolbar

2   Select the **Crop** tool ⊹, position it over a handle and drag towards the middle of the picture. Experiment with a different handle to see how it works. Try uncropping it by dragging the same handle outwards again and then crop it once more.

3   Crop the picture in the bottom right corner.

4   Select each picture in turn and click on the **Line Style** ☰ button to add a border.

5   Create a text box on the first picture and key in **Original**.

6   Fill the box with a colour that will show on the picture. Rotate the text box so that it slopes upwards from left to right by **45°** (key in −45°) and make it **semitransparent** (set transparency to 50%).

7   Create a text box on the cropped picture below and key in **Cropped**. Fill the box with a colour that will show on the picture. Rotate the text box so that it slopes downwards from right to left by **45°** and make it **semitransparent**.

Remember:

To rotate by a specific angle select the text box, then use **Format – Text Box – Size**.

To make a colour semitransparent use **Format – Text Box – Colour and Lines**.

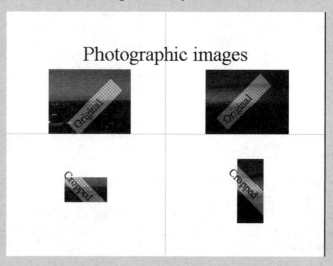

Figure 7.4 Example

Hint:

Use **Draw** on the **Drawing** toolbar and **Order** if necessary.

8   Label the pictures on the right in the same way. The slide should resemble Figure 7.4.
9   Save.

Information: Inserting an image from a web browser

When using images from an intranet or the Internet you should consider the question of copyright as you may be breaking copyright law. This also applies to the text you used in Section 5. Copyright means that the creator or owner has the right to control who can make copies of their work and how it can be used. Some sites may allow you to use their material if it is for personal use, i.e. not for commercial purposes. Some may request that an acknowledgement is given as to its source.

There are two ways of inserting an image from a web browser. One is to save it and insert it as you did in Task 7.1. The other is simply to copy and paste it. Using the first method means that you have an image file saved for future use. With copying and pasting you do not, although you can always copy and paste it from one slide or presentation to another.

You can use the Internet or your college intranet for this task. If you load your favourite search engine and search for '**free photographs**' you should be able to find some suitable sites.

Task 7.3	**Save and insert an image from a web browser**

Method

1   Load your intranet or Internet web browser and locate an image.
2   Position the mouse pointer over the picture and click the **right** mouse button.
3   Using the **left** mouse button select **Save Picture As** (Figure 7.5).

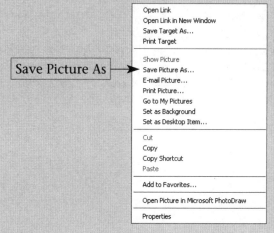

Figure 7.5 Save Picture As

Hint:

Notice you can copy a picture and then paste it into a slide.

4   The default location for saving images is a folder called My Pictures. To save it to a different folder, click on **My Documents** and select the folder **Presentation Graphics Level 2**. Key in a suitable filename and click **Save**.

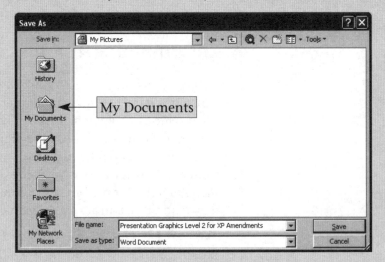

Figure 7.6 Save Picture

5   Using the same presentation as for the previous task, insert a new **Title Only** slide and key in the heading **Images from the Internet**.

6   The image will be inserted in the same way as you did in Task 7.1 – select **Picture** from the **Insert** menu and then **From File**. Locate the folder **Presentation Graphics Level 2** and the image you just saved. Click on **Insert**.

7   Position the image of the left side of the slide, resizing if necessary. Save.

Task 7.4 | **Copy and paste an image from a web browser**

Method

1	With the presentation still open on the same slide, load your intranet or Internet web browser and locate another image.
2	Click the **right** mouse button on the image and select **Copy**.
3	Switch back to the presentation using the task bar at the bottom of the screen.
4	Select **Paste** from the **Edit** menu.
5	Position the image on the right of the slide and resize if necessary.
6	Save.

| Task 7.5 | Specify position of object on a slide |

Method

1   Insert a new **Title Only** slide and key in the heading **Position objects**.
2   Copy one of the original images on slide 2 and paste it twice onto the new slide.
3   Select one of the images, choose **Picture** from the **Format** menu and then the **Position** tab.
4   Key in **5** in the Horizontal box – you do not need to key in cm (Figure 7.7).
5   Key in **5** in the Vertical box and click **OK**.

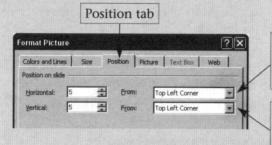

Position tab

Positions left edge of object **horizontally** by given measurement from this point

Positions object **vertically** by given measurement from this point

Figure 7.7 Position object

6   Select the second image, choose **Picture** from the **Format** menu and select the **Position** tab.
7   Key in **1** in the **Horizontal** box and click on the dropdown arrow beside the **From** box and choose **Centre**.
8   Key in **2** in the **Vertical** box and click on the dropdown arrow beside the **From** box and choose **Centre**.
9   Click **OK**.
10 Save.

Method

1   Using the same presentation select **Background** from the **Format** menu.
2   Click on the dropdown arrow and select **Fill Effects** (Figure 7.8).

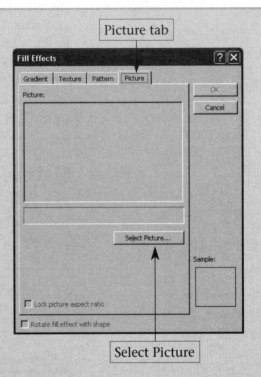

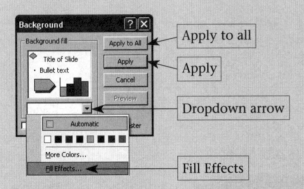

Figure 7.8 Format background

Figure 7.9 Fill Effects

3   Click on the **Picture** tab and **Select Picture** (Figure 7.9).
4   Locate the picture you require as you did in Task 7.1 and click **Insert**.
5   Click **OK** (Figure 7.10).

Figure 7.10 Select Picture

6   Click on **Apply to All** (Figure 7.8).
7   Save and print as handouts, four to a page.

Hint:

Apply to All affects all slides. **Apply** affects the current slide only.

Information: Other types of image file

Apart from photographic images there are other types of image you can use in a presentation. Examples are computer-drawn images using drawing programs and paint type programs. Whilst you can scan and import photographic images, you can actually scan anything that can be laid on a scanner, such as hand-drawn pictures and diagrams.

Things to do

1   Check to see what drawing/paint software you have available. You probably have Paint which is found by clicking on **Start – Programs – Accessories – Paint**. Try some of the tools in the left-hand toolbox – some are used in a similar way to those on the Drawing toolbar in PowerPoint. Save an image (it does not matter how basic it is!) and then insert it into a PowerPoint slide. Try creating and saving another image and using it in the background.

2   Do you have access to a scanner? If so, scan a photograph and save it. Hand draw a simple picture or a diagram (perhaps a room layout). Scan it and save it. Experiment inserting a scanned image onto a slide and also using one in the background.

3   Find some images on the Internet on a topic of your choice, e.g. a place, an actor/actress, musician, etc. Save the images and put together a presentation using them, adding some relevant information to each slide.

→ Practise your skills 7.1

For this task you will need access to the Internet and two or three image files, preferably of seaside/coastal scenes. If you have access to a scanner you could scan some holiday photographs for this purpose.

1   Open a new presentation with a **Title** slide and key in the heading **Work with Pictures**.

2   Save the presentation as **Work with Pictures** into the **Skills Practice Level 2** folder.

3   Insert a new blank slide.

4   Load an Internet browser and search for a picture of **Niagara Falls**. Save the picture to the **Skills Practice Level 2** folder with a suitable name.

5   Format the slide background to insert the picture, applying it to this one slide only.

6   Search for a second image of **Niagara Falls** and copy and paste it onto the slide.

7   Format the picture to a height of **6 cm**, locking aspect ratio, and add a $\frac{1}{4}$ **pt border**.

8   Position the picture so it is **2 cm horizontally** and **vertically** from the **top left corner** of the slide.

9 Search for a third image of **Niagara Falls** and copy and paste it onto the slide.

10 Format the picture to a height of **6 cm**, locking aspect ratio, and add a $\frac{1}{4}$ **pt border**.

11 Position the picture so it is **2 cm horizontally** and **vertically** from the **centre** of the slide.

12 Create a text label reading **Niagara Falls** with font size **40** and position it centrally on the slide using guides. Ensure the label can be read – choose a suitable font colour if necessary.

13 Rotate the label so it is sloping upwards from left to right at an angle of **30°** (−30°).

14 Insert another blank slide. Load an Internet browser and search for a picture of **whales**. Save the picture to the **Skills Practice Level 2** folder with a suitable name.

15 Format the slide background to insert the picture, applying it to this one slide only.

16 Search for a second image of **whales** and copy and paste it onto the slide. Repeat for a third and fourth image.

17 Arrange the pictures, one in each corner of the slide except for the bottom right corner. Crop the slides where you can and resize the pictures to suit the slide. Add a border to each image.

18 Insert a text label size **40** reading **The Whale Kingdom** and position it in the bottom right corner. Use **Free Rotate** to rotate the text box so that it slopes downwards from left to right. Ensure the label can be read – choose a suitable colour font if necessary.

19 Insert a new blank slide. You will need your image files of seaside/ coastal scenes.

20 Format the slide background to insert one of your pictures, applying it to this one slide only.

21 Insert three or four pictures onto the slide, resizing as necessary, and add a border to each.

22 Crop each one in an appropriate way. (This will depend on the picture content.)

23 Arrange the pictures where you wish on the slide.

24 Insert a text box and key in **By the Sea** formatting it to size **40** and **bold**. Position it where it can be read, if necessary changing its colour.

25 Move to the first slide and format the slide background to insert any picture, applying it to this one slide only. (You could use one you have used already.)

26 Ensure the text can be read – change its colour if necessary.

27 Save and print as handouts, four to a page. If you have access to a colour printer, print them in colour. Close the presentation.

→ Practise your skills 7.2

You will require two images from the Internet for this task. One you will save as an image file and the other will be copied and pasted.

1 Open your web browser and search for a photographic picture of a road to form the background of the presentation. Save it into the **Presentation Graphics Level 2** folder.

2 Open the presentation **Smarts Driving School** from the **Presentation Graphics Consolidation** folder.

3 Use the saved image as the background for the first slide only. Change the font colour if necessary to ensure the text can be read on the background.

4 Move to the last slide and insert a new **Title Only** slide. Key in the heading **Keep it Safe**.

5 Search the Internet for a picture of a car and copy and paste it onto the last slide.

6 Crop the picture and resize it to a height of **9 cm**, locking aspect ratio.

7 Add a border.

8 Using the guides, position the picture in the centre of the slide.

9 Save the presentation as **Smarts Driving School Version 3** into the **Skills Practice Level 2** folder.

10 Print as handouts, four to a page, in colour, if you have access to a colour printer.

→ Check your knowledge

1 State sources of photographic images that you might incorporate into a presentation.

2 If you want to import images from an external source such as the Internet, why is copyright an important consideration?

3 Describe two different ways of importing pictures from an intranet or the Internet.

4 How can you ensure an image stays in proportion when resizing it by dragging?

5 What is this tool and what is its purpose?

Charts

You will learn to:

- Create organisation charts
- Create charts/graphs

PowerPoint has two features for drawing charts – one is for creating organisation charts and the other allows you to draw charts or graphs from numerical data. A graphical representation is usually much easier and quicker to understand than words or numbers.

Information: Organisation charts

Organisation charts allow you to display the structure of an organisation showing who reports to whom. This is much easier to read and understand at a glance than a written explanation.

Task 8.1 Create an organisation chart

Method

1 Open a new presentation and key in the main title **Creating Charts**.
2 Save the presentation as **Creating Charts** into the **Presentation Graphics Level 2** folder.
3 Insert a new slide selecting the **Title and Organization Chart** layout (Figure 8.1).

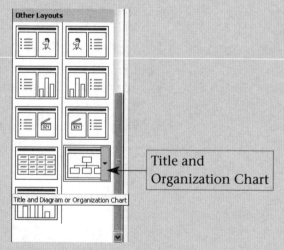

Figure 8.1 Title and Organization Chart layout

4 Double-click on the lower section of the slide (Figure 8.2). Microsoft Organization Chart opens in a new window.

Click to add title

Double click to add diagram or organization chart

Figure 8.2 Organisation chart

5 Select **Organization Chart** from the Diagram Gallery (Figure 8.3) and click **OK**.

Organization chart →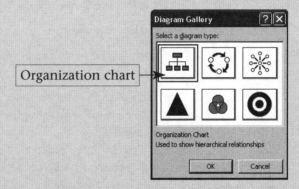

Figure 8.3 Diagram Gallery

6 A chart appears with text placeholders in each box (Figure 8.4). Click in the top box labelled **Click to add text** and key in **David Johnson**.

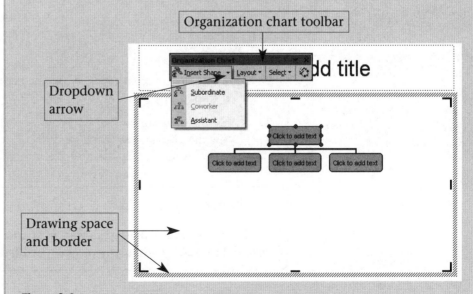

Figure 8.4 Organization Chart

7   Press **Enter** and key in **Managing Director**.
8   Click into the box on the left and key in **Paolo Rossi**.
9   Press **Enter** and key in **Office Manager**.
10   Click into the middle box and key in **Joni Bennett** with the title **HR Manager**.
11   Click into the last box and key in **Colin Pearson** with the title **Sales Manager**.

Adding a subordinate

Each level of an organisation chart is subordinate to the one above it. Therefore a person reporting to a manager in the example chart created above, would be a subordinate.

12   Click on the **HR Manager** box and then click on the down arrow by **Insert Shape** (Figure 8.4). Select **Subordinate**.
13   In the new box, key in **David Cox** with the title **HR Assistant**.
14   Click on the **Managing Director** box and click on **Insert Shape**.
15   In the new box, key in **Kirsten Jones** with the title **Technical Support**.

Deleting a box

16   Click on the edge of the **Sales Manager** box (small round handles appear) and press **Delete** on the keyboard.

Formatting the chart

The chart can be formatted in various ways including changing font, font size and colours.

17   Click on the chart drawing space and use Fill Color ![fill color icon] ▾ to choose a colour.
18   Click in the **Managing Director** box and use Fill Color ![fill color icon] ▾ to choose a colour.

19   To select the second level of boxes all at once, click in one of them and select **Level** from the **Select** menu on the Organization chart toolbar (Figure 8.5). Choose a fill colour.

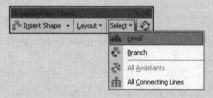

Figure 8.5 Selecting an entire level

Be aware that a chart could end up looking rather bright and gaudy and in practice it is best to keep it fairly simple.

20   Save the presentation.
21   View the presentation and close.

Hint:

To change the contents of a box, click on it and edit as normal.

Hint:

To edit a chart slide later, click on the drawing space (Figure 8.4) to display the chart toolbar.

Information

Although they are called organisation charts, these types of charts can also be used to display other structures with different levels of information.

Things to do

1 Open **Creating Charts**, insert a new **Title and Organization Chart** slide and experiment with Co-workers and Assistants to see how they work. See **Insert Shape** on the Organization chart toolbar.

2 Insert a new slide and create the chart as shown in Figure 8.6. You can make up the names to go in the boxes.

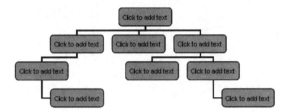

Figure 8.6 Sample chart

3 Change the font and font colour of all boxes.

4 Change the box colour and shadow of the second level.

5 Now amend the chart so that it looks like Figure 8.7.

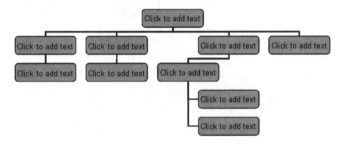

Figure 8.7 Sample chart 2

6 Try moving a box – point and drag a box over its new manager or co-worker.

7 Add the title **Sample Chart** and save the presentation.

Information: Charts and graphs

There is a saying that 'a picture speaks a thousand words'. Certainly charts or graphs present numerical data in a way that is much easier to understand at a glance than lots of numbers. Different charts are used for different purposes:

Bar or column chart	Used to show comparison between sets of numbers using horizontal bars or vertical columns
Line chart	Trends over a period of time are shown by drawing connecting lines between points
Pie chart	Percentage values are represented as slices of a pie

Task 8.2　Create a chart

Method

1　Using the same presentation insert a new slide selecting **Title and Chart** layout (Figure 8.8).

Figure 8.8 Title and Chart layout

2　Double-click on the slide – a datasheet and a sample chart appear.
3　Click in the top left corner of the datasheet (Figure 8.9) to select all the data and press **Delete** on the keyboard to clear the data.

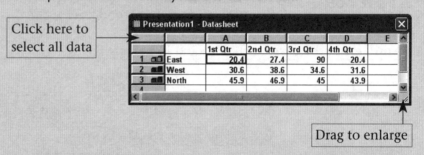

Figure 8.9 Datasheet

4　Key in the data as shown in Figure 8.9. Notice how the chart builds up as you do so.
5　Click on a blank area of the slide to return to Slide view.
6　Key in the title **Meals served**.

To return to chart and datasheet view
7　Double-click on the chart.

To change chart type
8　Click on the **Chart** menu and select **Chart Type**.
9　Click on **Line** chart and then **OK** (Figure 8.10).

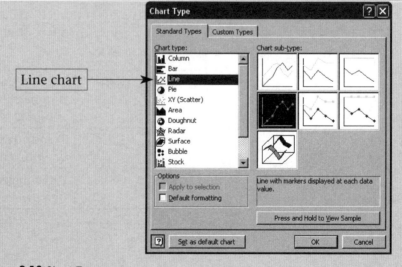

Figure 8.10 Chart Type

10   Click on the **Chart** menu again and select **Chart Type**.

11   Click on **Column** and then **OK**.

12   Click on a blank area of the slide to return to Slide view.

13   Insert a new **Chart** slide and double-click to add a chart.

14   Delete the data as you did before and key in the new data as shown in Figure 8.11.

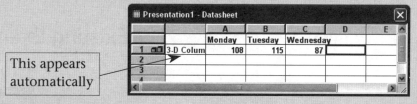

Figure 8.11 Create a pie chart

15   Click on the **Chart** menu and select **Chart Type**.

16   Click on **Pie** and then **OK**.

Adding labels

Whilst there is a key or legend, it would be useful to display labels on the pie chart.

17   Click on the **Chart** menu and choose **Chart Options**.

18   Click on the **Data Labels** tab (Figure 8.12) and then **Percentage**. Click **OK**.

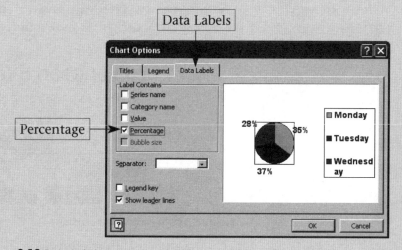

Figure 8.12 Data Labels

19   Click on a blank area of the slide and key in the title **Total Meals Sold**.

20   Save the presentation and print as handouts, six to a page.

21   View the presentation and close.

Information

If you are familiar with Excel and have created a chart within a spreadsheet, it can be copied and pasted onto a slide.

More graphical objects can be inserted onto a slide by selecting **Object** from the **Insert** menu and then choosing the type of object you require. However, this is likely to need knowledge of the software with which to create it and is therefore beyond the scope of this book.

→ Practise your skills 8.1

1 Open a new presentation with a **Title** slide. Add the title **Abney College** with the subtitle **Exams**.

2 Insert a new **Title and Organization Chart** slide and create a heading and chart as shown in Figure 8.13.

Existing Exams Office

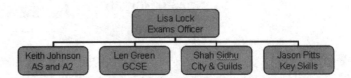

Figure 8.13 Existing Exams Office

3 Change the font of all boxes to **Times New Roman** and **italics**.

4 Change the colour of the top level box to a different colour with a shadow effect.

5 Insert a new **Title and Organization Chart** slide and create a heading and chart as shown in Figure 8.14.

Proposed Exams Office

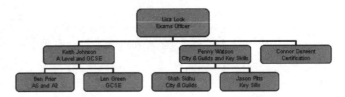

Figure 8.14 Proposed Exams Office

6 Make the text in the second level of boxes bold, fill those boxes with a different colour and apply a shadow.

7 Choose a design template for your slides.

8 Add a footer showing your name with a date that will update automatically, but no slide number. Footer information is not required on the Title slide.

9 Check the presentation, save as **Abney College** into the **Skills Practice Level 2** folder.

10 Print as handouts, three to a page, and close.

→ Practise your skills 8.2

1 Open the presentation **Abney College** from the **Skills Practice Level 2** folder.

2 Move to the last slide and insert a new **Chart** slide with a heading **Key Skills Results**. Create a chart based on the data in Figure 8.15.

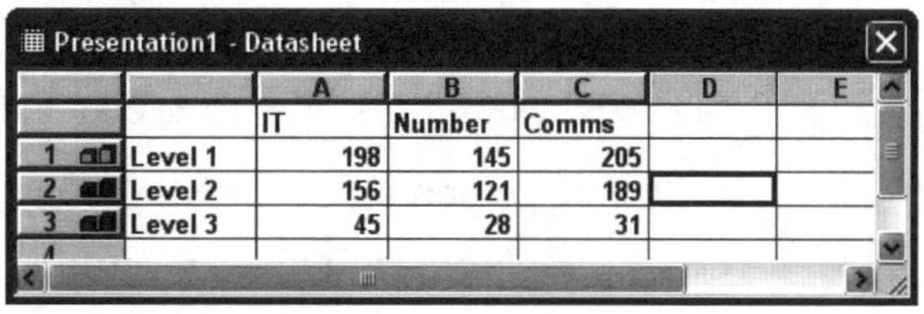

Presentation1 - Datasheet

		A	B	C	D	E
		IT	Number	Comms		
1	Level 1	198	145	205		
2	Level 2	156	121	189		
3	Level 3	45	28	31		

Figure 8.15 Key skills results chart

3 Insert a new **Chart** slide with a heading **Key Skills By Levels**. Create a chart based on the data in Figure 8.16.

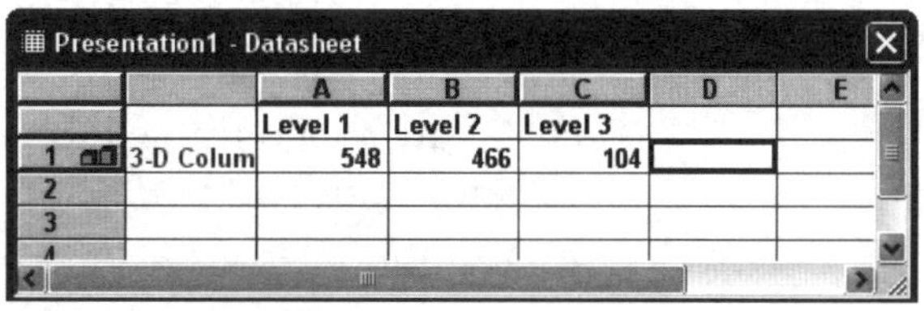

Presentation1 - Datasheet

		A	B	C	D	E
		Level 1	Level 2	Level 3		
1	3-D Colum	548	466	104		
2						
3						

Figure 8.16 Keys skills by levels

4 Save the presentation as **Abney College Version 2** into the **Skills Practice Level 2** folder.

5 Reopen the last slide and change it to a pie chart. Add labels showing the percentages.

6 Change the footer to also display the slide numbers.

7 Save the presentation and print as handouts, six to a page.

8 Close.

→ Check your knowledge

1 What are the two main types of chart used in this section?

2 What is the advantage of presenting a chart rather than a table of numbers?

3 What is the purpose of the following types of chart?

- Bar or column chart
- Line chart
- Pie chart

Consolidation 3

For this task you will need the text file **Newburch Motors**, which should be stored in the folder called **Text files**. If you do not have access to this file you should create it now (see Appendix). You will also need a photographic image of a road or motorway saved as an image file.

You are going to create a presentation for the Regional Manager of Newburch Motors to use at a staff update meeting.

1 Open a new blank presentation.

2 Format the background with a **two-colour gradient** effect using two pale colours with a **Horizontal** shading style applying to all slides.

3 On the Master slide change the title style and the text style to one of your choice. Change the text colour to one of your choice. Do the same for the footer items.

4 Change the bullet style to one of your choice.

5 Create a logo using a **Regular pentagon autoshape** with a height and width of **2 cm**. Fill it with a pale colour.

6 Use WordArt to create the letter **N**, resize it and position inside the shape created above.

7 Group the two objects together.

8 Position the logo **0.4 cm horizontally** and **vertically** from the top left corner.

9 Insert a new Title Master.

10 On the Title Master resize the logo to **4 cm** high, locking aspect ratio.

11 Move the image to the middle of the slide above the title and using the ruler and guide, ensure it is in the centre.

12 Embolden the title and subtitle.

13 Change to Normal view and key in the title **Newburch Motors**.

14 Insert a footer to show the date to update automatically, the slide number and your name. (Choose a **date style**.) The footer is not required on the Title slide.

15 Insert a header on **Notes and Handouts** to display your name with the date and page number.

16 Save the file as a design template with the name **Newburch Motors**.

17 Close the template file.

18 Open a copy of the new template.

19 Add the subtitle **The Road Ahead** to the Title slide.

20 Using **Slides from Outline** on the **Insert** menu, import the text file **Newburch Motors** from the **Text files** folder.

21 Using **Demote/Promote**, organise the slides as shown in Figure 8.17.

22 Save the presentation as **The Road Ahead** into the **Presentation Graphics Consolidation** folder.

23 Insert a new blank slide as the last slide and format the background of this one slide with your image of a road or motorway.

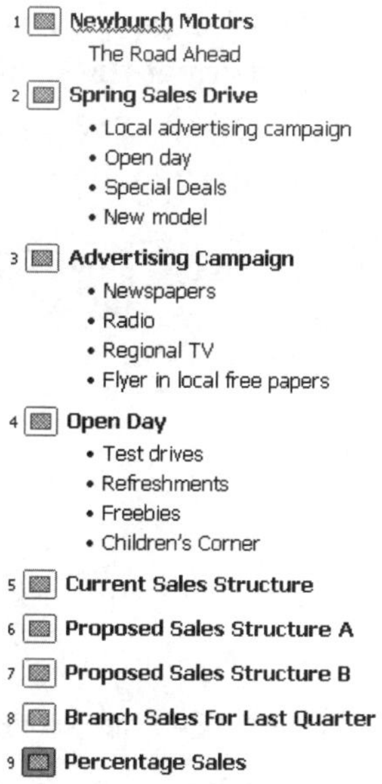

1 Newburch Motors
The Road Ahead
2 Spring Sales Drive
• Local advertising campaign
• Open day
• Special Deals
• New model
3 Advertising Campaign
• Newspapers
• Radio
• Regional TV
• Flyer in local free papers
4 Open Day
• Test drives
• Refreshments
• Freebies
• Children's Corner
5 Current Sales Structure
6 Proposed Sales Structure A
7 Proposed Sales Structure B
8 Branch Sales For Last Quarter
9 Percentage Sales

Figure 8.17 Outline

24 Insert a text box with the words **Where are we going?** Increase the text size to **36** and fill the background of the text box with a pale colour and make it **semitransparent** (50%).

25 Position the text box in the centre of the page and then rotate it by $-$**20°** so it is sloping upwards from left to right.

26 Slide 2 layout should be changed to **Title, Text and Clip Art**. Add suitable clip art.

27 Repeat for slides 3 and 4.

28 On the **Current Sales Structure** slide create the organisation chart in Figure 8.18.

Current Sales Structure
John Clifford
Sales Director
Jay Connor
Southern
Lucy Dawson
Midlands
Kevin Dean
London

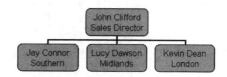

Figure 8.18 Current Sales Structure

29 On the **Proposed Sales Structure A** slide create the organisation chart in Figure 8.19.

Proposed Sales Structure A
John Clifford
Sales Director
Jay Connor
Southern
Lucy Dawson
Midlands
Kevin Dean
London
TBA
Lease Vehicles
TBA
Hire Vehicles

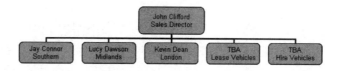

Figure 8.19 Proposed Sales Structure A

30 Change the colour of the two **TBA** boxes and add a shadow effect. Format the text as italics.

31 On the **Proposed Sales Structure B** slide create the organisation chart in Figure 8.20.

Proposed Sales Structure B

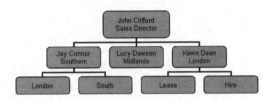

Figure 8.20 Proposed Sales Structure B

32 Change the colour of the **Jay Connor** and the **Kevin Dean** boxes and add a shadow effect. Format the text as italics.

33 Change the layout of the **Branch Sales for Last Quarter** slide to a Chart layout and create a column chart using the data in Figure 8.21.

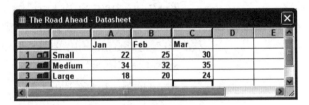

Figure 8.21 Sales datasheet

34 Change the layout of the **Percentage Sales** slide to a Chart layout and create a pie chart using the data in Figure 8.22.

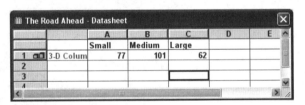

Figure 8.22 Percentage sales datasheet

35 Add percentage labels to the chart.

36 Check the presentation and save.

37 In slide sorter move the slide with the background image to become slide 2.

38 Print as handouts, six to a page.

39 Print slide 2 as a slide.

40 Save.

Section 9   Special effects

You will learn to:

- Add slide transition effects
- Animate objects on slides
- Insert animations
- Insert sound files

Special effects can be added to presentations to make them visually and audibly more interesting. These include transition effects – the way in which one slide changes to another – animation and sound effects. However, you can overdo it, so be selective in their use.

Information: Slide transition effects

Transition effects are special effects that introduce a slide. There are a variety of effects to choose from.

Task 9.1   Apply slide transition effects

Method

1   Open the presentation **Smarts Driving School Version 2** from the **Presentation Graphics Consolidation** folder. (Your slides are likely to have a different design template background to the examples shown below.)
2   Save the presentation straight away as **Smarts with animation** into the **Presentation Graphics Level 2** folder.
3   Switch to Slide Sorter view and select the first slide.
4   Click on the **Slide Transition button** ⊞ Transition on the Slide Sorter toolbar. The Slide Transition task pane opens. (Figure 9.1). Choose any effect from the list. An effect is applied to the slide and previews as you select it.

Hint:

You can also set transition effects in Normal or Slide Sorter view using **Slide Transition** on the **Slide Show** menu.

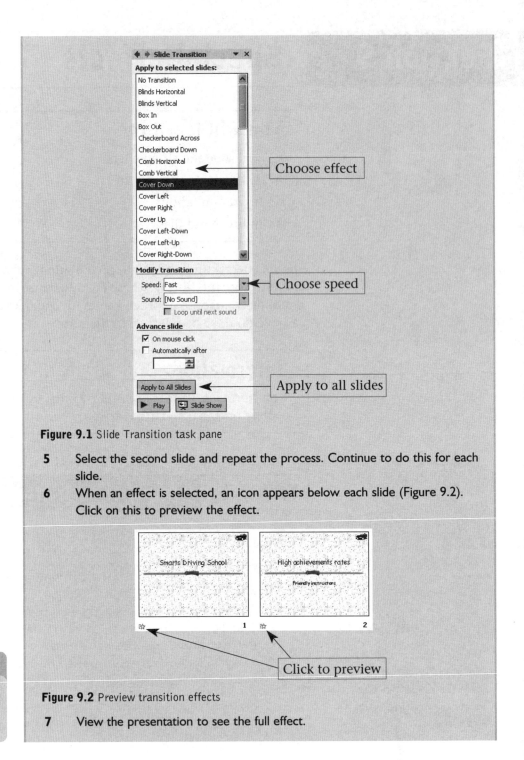

Figure 9.1 Slide Transition task pane

5 Select the second slide and repeat the process. Continue to do this for each slide.

6 When an effect is selected, an icon appears below each slide (Figure 9.2). Click on this to preview the effect.

Figure 9.2 Preview transition effects

7 View the presentation to see the full effect.

Information: Presentation or slideshow?

These two terms are fairly interchangeable. A presentation, however, is likely to be controlled manually by a speaker who advances each slide when he or she is ready. A slideshow might better describe a series of slides that are set to run automatically without the need for anyone to control them. You will do this in the next section.

Information: Choosing effects

If you have chosen many different effects, it can be rather distracting, and, although it does depend on the purpose of the presentation, it is usually best to keep it fairly simple. You should aim to draw attention to the slides, not to the effects themselves. You could use two simple effects alternately or apply one effect to all slides. The speed can also be changed.

Hint:

You can also choose **Select All** from the **Edit** menu and then apply an effect to all slides.

8   Click on the **Speed** dropdown arrow in the task pane and select **Slow** (Figure 9.1).
9   Click on **Apply to All**.
10   Save and view the presentation.

Information: Animation

Animation can be added to objects and affects the way they behave as they appear on a slide. Bear in mind the audience you are preparing the presentation for. Some animation effects are simple, others are more eye-catching and even distracting. If it is a serious subject, certain animation effects may not be appropriate, whereas if you are trying to inject some humour, then it might be. **Animation** can be used to bring in each object on a slide separately, including clip art and bullet points. This can be very useful for introducing bullet points one after the other as it means that the audience can concentrate on one point at a time, rather than trying to read them all at once.

Task 9.2	Apply an animation scheme

Method

1   Select **Animation Schemes** from the **Slide Show** menu. (The task pane opens.)
2   Select one of the slides with bullets.
3   Select an animation effect from the task pane (Figure 9.3).

Figure 9.3 Animation

4   To apply to all slides, click on **Apply to All**.
5   Save the presentation and then view it. You will need to click the mouse or press **Enter** for each clip art object and bullet point to appear.

Information: Custom animation

Custom animation gives you more control over the animation of slide objects as an animation effect can be applied to a single object. Charts can be animated, so that, for example, the bars of a column chart will display one by one. The order in which objects appear on a slide can also be controlled. If you really want to distract the audience there are also some simple sound effects! As with slide transition effects, do be selective and think about the audience who may have to watch a busy, flashy slideshow with (maybe) annoying sound effects. A sound effect, however, could be used to grab the audience's attention.

Task 9.3   Apply custom animation

Method

1   Switch to **Normal** view and move to a slide with clip art and bullets.
2   Select **Custom Animation** from the **Slide Show** menu (not available in Slide Sorter view).
3   Click on the clip art image and then click on **Add Effect** (Figure 9.4).

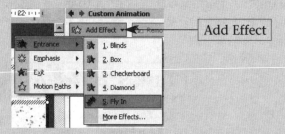

Figure 9.4 Custom animation

4   From the side menu select **Entrance** and then choose an effect from the second side menu. Select **More Effects** for further choices.
5   Click on the title and then click on **Add Effect**. Choose an Entrance effect as before. Notice how a numbered tag appears beside these objects showing the order in which the effects will play.
6   Click on **Play** (Figure 9.5). The animation scheme you applied first plays before the custom animation effects.

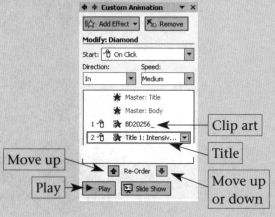

Figure 9.5 Change order

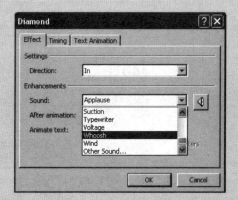

Figure 9.6 Sound effect

7   To change the order of play, click on the **Title** in the task pane and then click on the **Re-order** button to move up.

8   Click on **Play** again to see the change.

9   To add a sound effect click on the dropdown arrow beside **Title** in the task pane and select **Effect Options**.

10 Select a sound effect from the Sound dropdown list (Figure 9.6).

11 Save and view the presentation.

Things to do

Apply custom animation to each slide in this presentation. Ensure that the title effect comes in first, followed by clip art objects and then bulleted text. (Clip art that has been placed on the Master slide appears as part of the background, although this too could be animated in Slide Master/Title Master view.) When complete, save and view the slideshow.

Information: Animating charts

Bringing in each column of a chart separately is a useful way of gradually building up to reveal an overall picture to an audience.

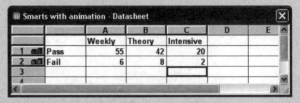

Task 9.4   Animate a chart

Method

I   Insert a new **Title and Chart** slide as the last slide with a title **First-time pass rates** and create a chart based on the datasheet in Figure 9.7.

Smarts with animation - Datasheet

		A Weekly	B Theory	C Intensive	D	E
1	Pass	55	42	20		
2	Fail	6	8	2		
3						
4						

Figure 9.7 Datasheet

2   Click on the chart. If the **Custom Animation** task pane is not open, select it from the **Slide Show** menu.

3   Click on **Add Effects** and choose **Entrance**. Select **More Effects** and then **Appear**. Click **OK**.

4   In the task pane click on the dropdown list beside the chart animation effect and choose **Effect Options**.

5   Select the **Chart Animation** tab (Figure 9.8) and **By category** from the dropdown list. Click **OK**.

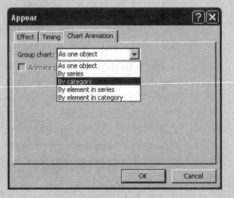

Figure 9.8 Chart animation

Hint:

Pie charts can also be animated but only by **Category**.

6   Click on **Play** in the task pane to preview the effect.

7   Experiment with the other chart animation options as seen in Figure 9.8, ending with **By category**.

8   Save and view the presentation.

Information: Multimedia objects

Multimedia objects, such as animations, sound files, video and music, can be inserted into PowerPoint slides. The following file types are examples of those that are supplied with PowerPoint. You can, however, insert similar files created elsewhere. The Internet is a source of copyright-free animated gif files, for example. These are little cartoon-like animations.

Animated picture	gif	(Graphics Interchange Format)
Sound	midi	(Musical Instrument Digital Interface)
Sound	wma	(Windows Media Audio)
Video	avi	(Audio Video Interleave)

Method

1   Insert a new **Title Only** slide as the last slide and insert the heading **And finally ...**

2   Use WordArt to create the text **Succeed with Smarts**. Fill the WordArt with a colour that matches the colour scheme of the background. Position below the heading.

3   From the **Insert** menu select **Movies and Sound**. From the side menu select **Movie from Clip Organizer**. The Insert Clip Art task pane opens (Figure 9.9).

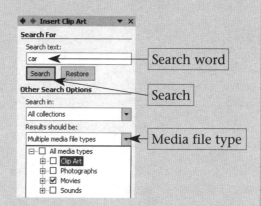

Figure 9.9 Insert an animation   **Figure 9.10** Search for animation or movie

4   Scroll through the task pane list to look for a suitable clip. Click on one to select it. Depending on the file type selected, a message may appear asking if you want the movie to play automatically (when the slideshow is viewed). Click on **Yes**. If you choose **No** it will only play when you click it as the slide loads. **Note:** Animations and movies only play when slides are viewed.

5   Position the image and view the presentation – the movie should start playing automatically when the slide loads.

6   Another way of finding a suitable animation is to search for it. Return to the last slide and click on **Insert Clip Art** 🖼️ . The task pane appears (Figure 9.10).

7   Key in the search word **car** and click on the dropdown arrow below **Results should be:**. (Try another search word if this does not produce any results.)

8   Click in the check box by **movies**. Remove any other checkmarks if present. Click on **Search**.

9   Select an image as before and position on the slide.

10   Save and view the presentation.

Method

1   Move to the first slide and select **Movies and Sounds** from the **Insert** menu.
2   From the side menu select **Sound from Clip Organizer** (Figure 9.11).

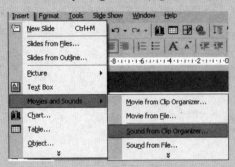

Figure 9.11 Insert sound

3   The Insert Clip Art task pane opens (Figure 9.12). Click on the side bar of a sound object and select **Preview**.

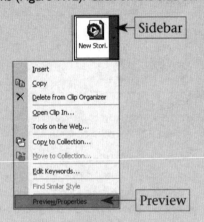

Figure 9.12 Preview sound

4   The Preview window opens (Figure 9.13) and the sound starts to play. Click on the **Stop** button when ready and close the window. Repeat with another sound until you have found one you want to use.

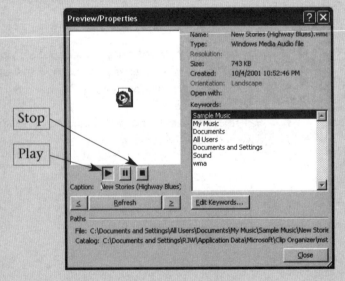

Figure 9.13 Preview sound 2

5   To insert a sound file onto the slide select it in the task pane.

6 The following dialogue box appears. This means that if you click **Yes**, the sound will play automatically when the slide on which it is inserted appears in the slideshow. If you click **No** it will only play when the slideshow is viewed if you click on the sound icon. Click **Yes**. The sound icon 🔊 appears on the slide.

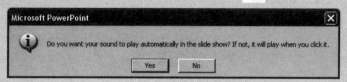

Figure 9.14 Play sound automatically

7 Save and view the presentation. The sound will play on the first slide until you move to the next.
8 On the last slide insert a sound clicking **No** when the dialogue box in Figure 9.14 appears.
9 Save and view the presentation. You will need to click on the sound icon when you reach the last slide to make it play.

Hint:

To remove a sound, delete the sound icon on the slide.

Task 9.7	Control sound

You may be required to play a sound throughout a presentation and you will need to use Custom Animation to set this up.

Method

1 In **Normal** view move to the first slide and select **Custom Animation** from the **Slide show** menu or right click on the sound icon and choose **Custom Animation**. The Custom Animation task pane opens.
2 Select the sound object in the task pane list and click on the dropdown list. Choose **Effect Options** (Figure 9.15).

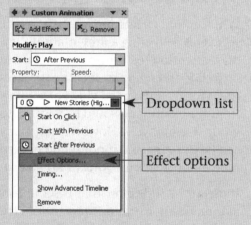

Figure 9.15 Effect options

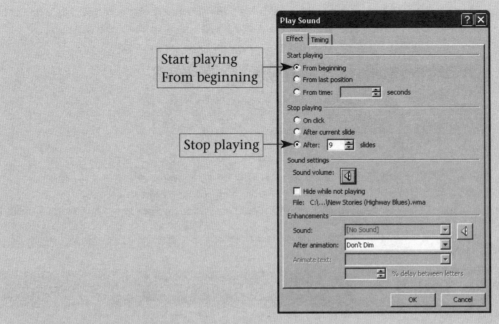

Start playing
From beginning

Stop playing

Figure 9.16 Play sound settings

3   Click on Start playing **From beginning** if not already selected.
4   Click on Stop playing **After** and key in **9** (being the last slide). Click **OK**.
5   Save and view the slideshow. Click the mouse to start the sound.
    Demonstrate it to your tutor.

Information: Using effects and multimedia

Whilst sound effects and animations should be used with care, when a speaker is delivering a presentation they can be used very sparingly to draw attention to or introduce a particular point. One might be placed on a slide and set up so that the speaker can click to start it when he or she is ready. A recorded video or sound file with, for example, a message from the chairman, would be very relevant for a presentation given to a group of employees. However, too many sound and animation effects can be irritating and if not set up properly might play at the wrong moment, play for too long or not play at all when required.

If used for a slideshow that is set to run continuously and automatically without intervention, the same comments about effects apply. A video clip could be useful though, as could sound in the form of a recorded commentary or even an unobtrusive soundtrack.

Whilst practising your new skills you may use many different effects. However, when creating presentations or slideshows for a real purpose, do not fall into the trap of many new users who become so excited by effects that they use every trick in the book!

Information: Screenshots

You may be asked to produce a screenshot or screen dump to provide evidence of your work. This is effectively a copy of what is on your screen at the time. You will need access to Word for this task.

Task 9.8   Create a screenshot

Method

I   Switch to **Slide Sorter** view and press the **Print Screen** button on the right-hand side on the top row of the keyboard (Figure 9.17).

Figure 9.17 Print Screen button

2   Open a new **Word** document and key in your name.

3   Select **Paste** from the **Edit** menu or click on the **Paste** button 📋.

4   Save as **Smarts screenshot** in **Skills Practice Level 2** folder, print and close.

Hint:

Pressing **Print Screen** copies an image of the screen to the **Clipboard**, the area of Windows memory that holds information until you are ready to paste it elsewhere. You could also use **WordPad** or **Paint** to paste the screenshot.

Things to do

If you have access to the Internet try a search for **free animated gifs** and save them to insert in a presentation. You could also look for sound files – search for **free sound files**. These files can be saved to My documents and inserted by selecting **Sound and Movies** from the **Insert** menu and **From file**.

→ Practise your skills 9.1

1   Open the file **The Road Ahead** from the **Presentation Graphics Consolidation** folder.

2   Save it as **The Road Ahead with Animation** into the same folder.

3   Apply the slide transition **Cover Left** to all slides and set the speed to **Medium**.

4   Apply **Custom Animation** to each slide so that the title appears first, followed by the text and then any graphic.

5   The column chart should be animated so that each element appears **by Series**.

6   The pie chart should be animated so that each element appears **by Category**.

7   Apply a sound effect that will play throughout.

8   Produce a screenshot of the slides in **Slide Sorter** view pasted into Word. Add your name.

9   Save as **The Road Ahead Screenshot** into **Skills Practice Level 2** folder and view the presentation.

10   Demonstrate the presentation to your tutor and then close.

→ Practise your skills 9.2

1 Open the **Abney College Version 2** presentation from the **Skills Practice level 2** folder.

2 Save it as **Abney College with Animation** into the same folder.

3 Apply the slide transition **Wipe Down** to all slides.

4 Apply **Custom Animation** to each slide so that the title appears first, followed by any other object.

5 The column chart should be animated so that each element appears **by Element in Series**.

6 The pie chart should be animated so that each element appears **by Category**.

7 Insert a sound that will only play when the sound icon is clicked, on each slide. Position the icon in the top right corner of the slides.

8 Produce a screenshot of the slides in Slide Sorter view pasted into Word. Add your name and print.

9 Save as **Abney College Screenshot** into the **Skills Practice Level 2** folder and view the presentation.

10 Demonstrate the presentation to your tutor and then close.

→ Check your knowledge

1 What feature is applied to affect the way in which one slide changes to another?

2 What feature is applied that affects the way text and objects appear on a slide? Describe some of its options.

3 Give examples of types of multimedia that can be inserted into slides.

4 What is the difference between a presentation and a slideshow?

5 What are the advantages and disadvantages of inserting multimedia objects into a presentation?

6 What are the advantages and disadvantages of inserting multimedia objects into a slideshow?

You will learn to:

- Create notes pages
- Look at further print options
- Create Summary slides
- Copy, delete and rearrange slides
- Hide a slide
- Add timings
- Create looped slideshows
- Save a presentation as a show
- Save a presentation with a viewer using Pack and Go

In this final section you will put the finishing touches to slides in a variety of ways. You will also add timings, so that a presentation can run as a looping slideshow, and prepare a presentation or slideshow to run on a computer without PowerPoint.

Information: Notes pages

When you are preparing a presentation that will be delivered to an audience, the slides will give you the basic outline of what you want to say. You probably won't be able to put everything you want to say onto the slides however, and notes are a useful aid to prompt you to say everything you need to. These can be added to slides and then printed to give you the prompts you need.

Task 10.1   Create notes

Method

I	Open **Abney College with Animation** from the **Skills Practice Level 2** folder.
2	Save it as **Abney College with Notes** into the same folder.
3	Move to slide 2 and switch to Normal view, if not currently displayed.
4	The Notes pane is below the Slide window (Figure 10.1). You can drag the boundary upwards to make the pane bigger if you need to.

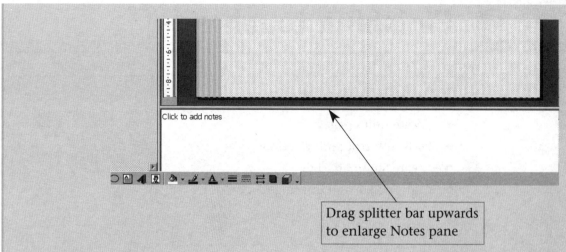

Drag splitter bar upwards to enlarge Notes pane

Figure 10.1 Notes pane

5 Click into the Notes pane and key in the following notes:
Shows current structure.
Each member of staff has responsibility for a different exam/exam type or exam board.

6 Move to slide 3 and key in the following notes:
Due to current workloads it is proposed to introduce a new level of supervision.
Additional staff will be put into post from existing personnel.

7 Move to slide 4 and key in the following notes:
The highest pass rates in all key skills is at Level 1.
Number has the lowest number of passes but also has fewer entries.
Few students attempt Level 3.

8 Move to slide 5 and key in the following notes:
Virtually half of all entries are at Level 1 followed closely by Level 2.
Level 3 attracts just under 10%.

9 Check for accuracy and save the presentation.

Hint:

Notes can also be viewed and keyed in using **Notes Page**. Select this from the **View** menu.

Information

In the next task you will print slides in Notes format. This will print each slide on a separate page with the slide filling the top half of the page and the notes in the bottom half.

In an earlier section you saw that printing handouts three to a page and distributing them to your audience gives them space to make brief handwritten notes. If you expect them to make longer notes, you could always print and distribute the slides in Notes format.

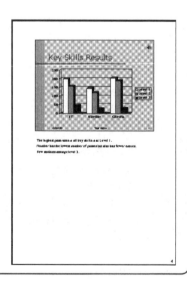

Notes printout

Method

I   To print notes, select **Print** from the **File** menu.

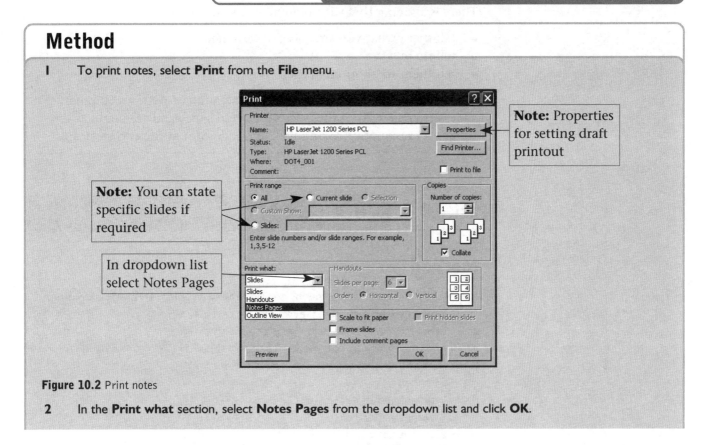

Figure 10.2 Print notes

2   In the **Print what** section, select **Notes Pages** from the dropdown list and click **OK**.

Information: Printing in black and white

Slides like these will display well when printed on a colour printer. However, they are often likely to be printed on a black and white (or monochrome) printer which means that colours will be printed in different shades of grey. If you do not want this to happen, select **Pure black and white** at the bottom of the printer dialogue box (hidden under dropdown list in Figure 10.2) to hide all shades of grey. Any objects with a fill colour will have no fill. This does not affect coloured clip art or photographic images which will still print with shades of grey. The problem with printing in black and white is that colours can look muddy and patterns may not be clear. Any colour used to distinguish, say, segments of a pie chart or parts of a diagram, will not show. Try printing one of the slides first with **Grayscale** checked and then in **Pure black and white**.

Information: Draft printing

When printing, it is possible with most printers to print a draft or a lower resolution copy. This saves ink or toner, which is expensive. The quality and resolution of a printout is measured in dots per inch (dpi). The higher the resolution, the more dots are used and therefore the level of detail is better. Printers have different features and you may be able to change the dpi and/or select an economy mode that saves toner. In the printer in Figure 10.2, draft mode is found by clicking on **Properties** and changing print quality. Experiment with your own printer to achieve draft printouts.

Information: Summary slides

There is a saying that with presentations you should:

- tell them what you are going to tell them
- tell them
- tell them what you told them!

A Summary slide could help with the first and last options. Summary slides are created from the titles of selected slides and are useful at the start of a presentation as an introduction and/or at the end to recap.

Task 10.3 — Create a Summary slide

Method

1. Close any open presentations and open **Smarts with Animation** from the **Presentation Graphics Level 2** folder.
2. Save as **Smarts with Summary** into the same folder.
3. Switch to **Slide Sorter** view. Hold down the **Ctrl** (Control) key and click on each of the following slides to select them:
   Services
   Intensive courses
   Theory preparation
   Practice tests
   First-time pass rates
   Other courses
4. Click on the **Summary Slide** button . The Summary slide appears in front of the first selected slide.

Task 10.4 — Copy, delete and rearrange slides

Hint:

You can also copy and paste a slide to duplicate it.

Remember:

You can also move slides in the Outline pane but it is easier to control in Slide Sorter view.

Method

1. Select the **Summary** slide and select **Duplicate** from the **Edit** menu.
2. Click on one of the **Summary** slides and drag it to become the last slide.
3. Click on the slide **And finally ...** and press **Delete** on the keyboard.
4. Save. Leave the presentation open.

Method

1   Open the presentation **The Road Ahead with Animation** from the **Skills Practice Level 2** folder.

2   Using slide sorter view select the slide with the photograph in the background and click on **Copy** .

3   Using the task bar at the bottom of the screen, click on **Smarts with Summary**.

Figure 10.3 Start menu

4   Click on **Paste** . The slide should appear. Move it to become the last new slide if necessary.

5   Change the text label to read **Where are you going?**

6   Save and view the presentation.

7   Print a draft Summary slide as a single slide.

8   Print all slides as draft handouts, nine to a page.

9   Leave both presentations open.

Hint:

Whilst a presentation is running a right-click of the mouse will show navigation options.

Information: Hiding a slide

Sometimes you may not want to use a slide in a particular presentation but you do not want to delete it as it will be needed later. In this case you can **Hide** a slide and it will not display when the slides are shown (until unhidden).

Task 10.6   Hide a slide

Hint:

In any other view, select **Hide Slide** from the **Slide Show** menu.

Method

1   Select the slide **High achievement rates** on the **Smarts with Summary** presentation.

2   In **Slide Sorter** view, click on the **Hide Slide** button . An icon appears below the slide on the right.

3   Save.

Task 10.7 — Framing a title and objects on a slide

A frame or border around a title and graphics may be used to enhance a slide and make it stand out from others.

Method

1. Switch to **The Road Ahead with Animation** presentation.
2. Move to the first slide and select the **Rectangle** tool ▢ .
3. Draw a rectangle around all objects on the slide.
4. Change the Fill to **No Fill**.
5. Change the colour to match the slide colour scheme and change the line thickness to **3 point**.
6. Using guides, ensure the frame is positioned in the centre across the page.
7. Print the first slide as a single slide in **Pure black and white**.
8. Save.

Information: Looped timed slideshows

In the last section you learnt that a **presentation** is the term usually used for a speaker giving a talk and moving through the slides manually with a mouse pointer, when he or she is ready for the next one to be viewed.

A **slideshow** will run on its own, looping continuously for as long as needed, for example for an exhibition or a college open evening. The best way to add timings to a slideshow is to rehearse them. This is like starting a timer that will record the timings for each slide. When you think a slide or slide object has been onscreen long enough for the audience to read or look at, you click to move on to the next one. Timings are then stored.

Task 10.8 — Rehearse timings

Method

1. Using **The Road Ahead with Animation**, select **Rehearse Timings** from the **Slide Show** menu. The presentation starts. Click the mouse or press **Enter** to bring in each new object or slide, making sure you leave enough time for the text to be read.
2. When you reach the end, the following screen appears (Figure 10.4). Click **Yes**. Timings can be seen below each slide.
3. Save.

Hint:

In **Slide Sorter** view click on the **Slide Transition** button 🔁 .

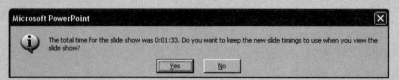

Figure 10.4 Save timings

Task 10.9 — Change timing on a slide

If after rehearsing the slideshow you feel that the timing of a slide is too fast, you can change it manually. In fact you can set all timings manually if you want to.

Hint:

In **Slide Sorter** view click on the **Slide Transition** button ⬚ Transition.

Method

1   Select a slide and then select **Slide Transition** from the **Slide Show** menu.
2   Change the number of seconds to **10** (Figure 10.5). You can key the number directly in you do not have to follow the default format. (If your timing is already 10, change it to 12.)

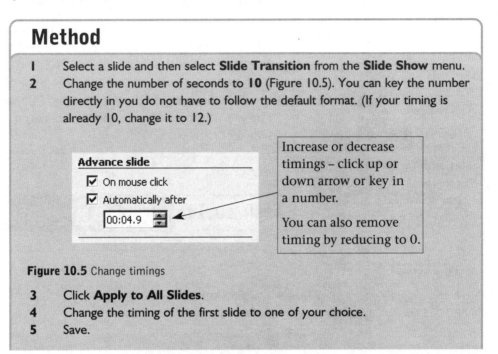

Figure 10.5 Change timings

3   Click **Apply to All Slides**.
4   Change the timing of the first slide to one of your choice.
5   Save.

Task 10.10 — Creating a looped show

Method

1   Select **Set Up Show** from the **Slide Show** menu.
2   Select **Loop continuously until 'Esc'** (i.e. until Esc is pressed) (Figure 10.6). Notice that **Using timings, if present** is selected.
3   Select **Browsed at a kiosk** which will loop continuously in a full screen display. Notice that Loop continuously is now unavailable.

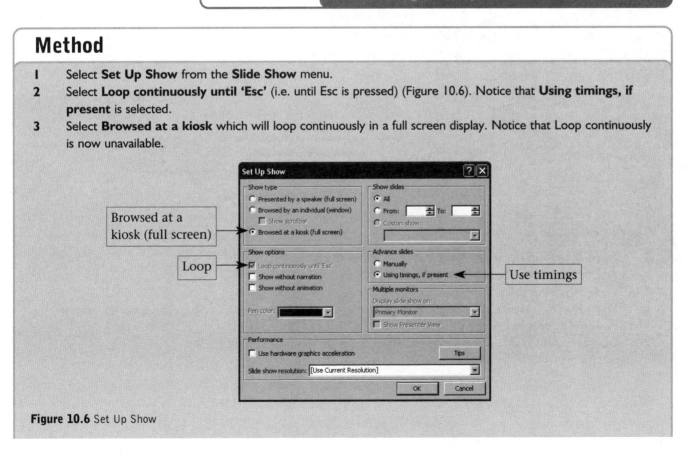

Figure 10.6 Set Up Show

4 Click **OK** and select **Slide Show** from the **View** menu. The slideshow starts to run. Let it run right through and start again and then press **Esc** when you are ready to stop it.

5 Save now to keep the new settings.

Information: Ways of saving a presentation

It is possible to save a presentation/slideshow in a way that packages it up with a viewer, so that it can be viewed on a computer that does not have PowerPoint. You might need to do this if you are giving a presentation or running a slideshow on a client's premises. This feature is called **Pack and Go**. It is also possible to save a presentation as a **show** so that it will play without having to open PowerPoint first. You will do this next.

Hint:

You can also save a presentation in other formats such as an earlier version of PowerPoint.

Task 10.11 | Save a presentation as a show

Method

1   Using the same presentation, select **Save As** from the **File** menu.
2   Click on **My Documents** (Figure 10.7) to save it in that location.

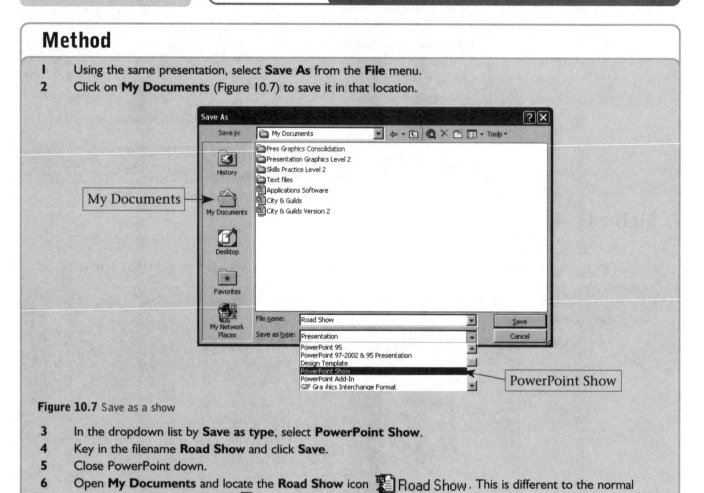

My Documents

PowerPoint Show

Figure 10.7 Save as a show

3   In the dropdown list by **Save as type**, select **PowerPoint Show**.
4   Key in the filename **Road Show** and click **Save**.
5   Close PowerPoint down.
6   Open **My Documents** and locate the **Road Show** icon 📑 Road Show . This is different to the normal PowerPoint presentation icon 📄.
7   Double-click to load it. Notice how you did not have to open PowerPoint first.

Now you will save a presentation with a viewer so that you could run it on a computer without PowerPoint.

Method

1   Load PowerPoint and open **Smarts with Summary** from the **Presentation Graphics Level 2** folder.
2   Select **Pack and Go** from the **File** menu. The Pack and Go Wizard starts.

Click **Next**

Figure 10.8 Pack and Go Step 1

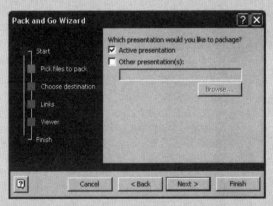

Check **Active presentation** (as this is the one currently open). Click **Next**

Figure 10.9 Pack and Go Step 2

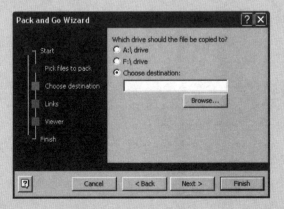

Select where you want to save the packed presentation – normally you would save it to A:/ drive (you would need several disks), to a CD, zip disk or flash drive to take it elsewhere

For practice purposes click **Choose destination** and **Browse**

Figure 10.10 Pack and Go Step 3

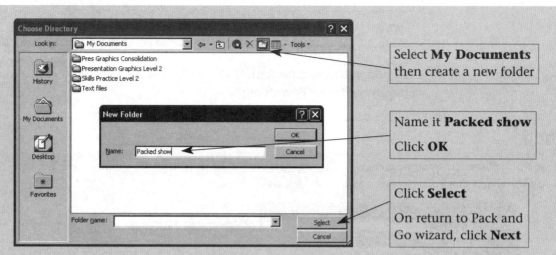

Select **My Documents** then create a new folder

Name it **Packed show**

Click **OK**

Click **Select**

On return to Pack and Go wizard, click **Next**

Figure 10.11 Select location

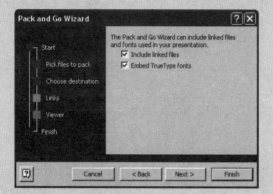

Check option to **Include linked files** and **Embed TrueType fonts** and click **Next**. This ensures that any sound files are included and fonts show correctly

Figure 10.12 Pack and Go Step 4

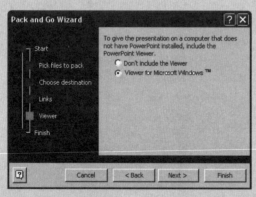

Check the option to include the Viewer and click **Next**

If the Viewer is not installed you may be prompted to do this first

Figure 10.13 Pack and Go Step 5

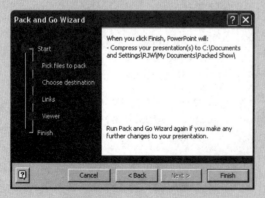

Click **Finish**

Figure 10.14 Pack and Go Step 6

3 Wait for the wizard to finish and then close PowerPoint. Look in the folder Packaged Show. You will see icons similar to the first two in Figure 10.15 – **PGNSETUP** and **PRES0.PPZ**. If you were to take this to run on another computer, you would need these two files on your disks, CD, zip disk or flash drive. The remaining icons are for normal presentations and a show.

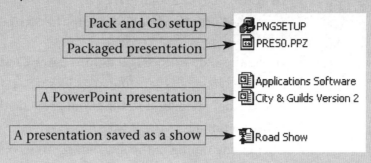

Figure 10.15 File icons

Information

To open up the packaged presentation on the destination computer you would need to open the file **Pngsetup.exe**. You would be asked for a destination folder and the files would be unpacked. You would then click on **Start** menu – **All Programs** and **Microsoft PowerPoint Viewer97** to load.

And finally . . .

Now you know how to create presentations and slideshows, but always think about your audience and what they will see.

Things to remember when creating slides

There are a number of things you should consider and this list is by no means exhaustive.

- Too much text on a slide – if there is more than about six lines of text divide into more than one slide.
- Text too small – make sure it is readable from a distance.
- Too many text colours – no more than two to a slide.
- Avoid fancy fonts – keep it simple.
- Ensure text can be read against the background.
- Spellcheck and check for accuracy.
- Use the Master slide to set fonts for consistency.
- Avoid all capital letters – they are hard to read.
- Avoid bright colours.
- Do not use too many different transition and animation effects – slides and objects flying in from all directions are confusing.
- Too many bullets can be boring.
- Ensure sufficient time is given to read each slide. This applies to both timed and manual presentations.

Ask yourself, do I want the audience to remember a flashy explosion of colour, sound and fancy effects, or the content of the presentation?

→ Practise your skills 10.1

1 Open **Smarts with Summary** from the **Presentation Graphics Level 2** folder.

2 Save it as **Smarts with Notes** into the **Skills Practice Level 2** folder.

3 Delete the slide titled **High achievement rates**.

4 Hide the second of the Summary slides (the last but one slide).

5 Add custom animation to the Summary slide that is not hidden.

6 Rehearse timings.

7 Change the timing of the last slide to **10** seconds. (If it is already 10 seconds, change it to 12.)

8 Set up the slideshow to loop continuously.

9 Add notes to the slides as shown:

Services

Courses tailored to your schedule and are available at all levels.

Intensive courses

Many people choose to learn with intensive tuition.

If you need to pass your test quickly and have the time to spare, this is the ideal method.

Theory preparation

Many people do not pass the theory test first time.

At Smarts we have it covered all ways, classroom sessions, computer-based practice just like the real thing.

Practice tests

The thought of the test makes people nervous.

With our practice test with a different instructor you won't be.

First-time pass rates

We have excellent first-time pass rates.

10 Move the slide containing the chart to become slide 3.

11 Save the slideshow.

12 Print as handouts, six to a page, in **Pure black and white**.

13 Save the slideshow again as a show that will run without opening PowerPoint first, into the **Skills Practice Level 2** folder using the name **Smart Startup**.

14 Produce a screenshot showing the files in the **Skills Practice Level 2** folder.

15 Close all files.

→ Practise your skills 10.2

1 Open the presentation **Winter Ailments Version 2** from the **Skills Practice Level 2** folder.

2 Create a Summary slide using all slides except the Title slide.

3 Duplicate the Summary slide and move the copy to become the last slide.

4 Change the page number in the footer of the master page to read **Page <#> of 8**.

5 Print the slides as handouts, nine to a page.

6 Save as **Winter Ailments with summary** into the same folder.

7 Save the presentation packaged with a viewer so that it can be viewed on a computer that does not have PowerPoint, using Pack and Go. Save into the same folder.

8 Produce a screenshot showing the files in the folder.

9 Close the file.

→ Check your knowledge

1 What is the problem with printing in black and white?

2 What is a Summary slide?

3 Why might you hide a slide?

4 Which views are used for rearranging slide order? Which is easiest?

5 Describe two ways of adding timings to slides.

6 For what purpose might you use a looped and timed slideshow?

7 For what purpose might you use a manually run presentation with a mouse pointer?

8 Why might a presentation be packaged with a viewer?

9 What is the feature used to do this?

10 How can you produce a presentation that will run without opening PowerPoint first?

Practice assignment

You are working for L Thornabys Supplies and a slideshow is required to show company procedures for e-mail and voice mail. You will need the text file **Procedures** (this may be supplied to you but can be created from the Appendix), three photographic image files related to the subject, e.g. a computer screen or someone working at a computer, a telephone, switchboard or person using the telephone. You may be given some images or you could find copyright-free images on the Internet. You could also create them yourself with a digital camera or scan existing pictures.

Task A

1 Create a new presentation.

2 On the Master slide change the title text to bold with right alignment.

3 Change the colour of all text to dark blue.

4 Change the bullet style for all levels of text to one of your choice.

5 Create a footer showing the date to update automatically, the slide number and an e-mail address as the footer text to read your_name@lthornabys.co.uk The footer is not required on the Title slide.

6 Format the background with a two-colour gradient fill using two pale colours with a shading style **From corner**.

7 Create a logo using the Trapezoid and Isosceles triangle shapes as well as WordArt in three different but toning colours.

8 Group these together and resize to a height and width of 2.5 cm. Position in the top left corner of the Master slide, 0.5 cm horizontally and vertically from the **top left corner**.

9 Import the text file **Procedures**.
   - Check the text for errors.
   - The lines with a number and a space are to be made slide headings.
   - The remaining lines should be indented to become bullets.
   - Delete the numbers from the slide headings.

10 On the first slide insert the title **Office Procedures**.

11 Copy the logo from the Master slide and paste it onto the first slide. Increase its size by 200% maintaining its proportion and position it on the right 1 cm below the horizontal centre line of the slide.

12 Save with the filename **Office Procedures Version 1** in a new folder called **Thornabys**.

Task B

1 Insert suitable clip art for slide 2 and resize it to fit alongside the text.

2 Insert a suitable picture into the background of the Voice Mail slide. Change the colour of the title on this slide if necessary, so that it is readable.

3 Insert a text box on this slide and enter the following text in capitals:

DO NOT USE VOICEMAIL TO AVOID ANSWERING THE TELEPHONE

4 Fill this text box with a white background and make it semitransparent (set to 50%). Rotate this box so that it is sloping upwards from left to right by 30°.

5 Insert a photographic image on slide 6, crop it and place it on the right-hand side so it is centred vertically.

6 Insert a Chart slide as the last slide with a slide title **Call response** and use the data below to create a pie chart with percentage labels.

5 rings	10 rings	15 rings
30	60	10

7 Insert a Title Only slide and key in the title **Call Routing**. Create the diagram below:

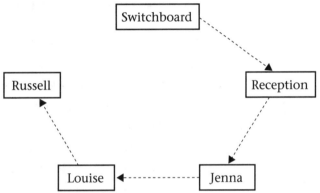

8 Add notes to slides as follows

Slide 4 Voice mail

Staff must not use voicemail to avoid taking calls at busy times

Slide 7 Call response

Currently only 30% of calls are answered within 5 rings

Aim is to bring this up to 50%.

Slide 8 Call routing

At busy times calls not answered within 5 rings will be automatically re-routed following this diagram

9 Produce a Summary slide using all slides except the first slide.

10 Save with the same name and print handouts, nine to a page. Label your printout **Printout 1**.

11 Produce a printout of the Call routing slide in Notes Pages format. Label your printout **Printout 2**.

Task C

1 Add a single transition effect to all slides with a medium speed.

2 Apply animation to all slides with bullets with the effect **Fly In**. Animation should not be applied to the titles or any images. (Apply Custom Animation to the bulleted text boxes.)

3 Animate the chart so the segments appear **by category**.

4 Add timings to all slides.

5 Add sound to the first slide that will play throughout the show.

6 Flip the clip art image on the E-mail etiquette slide so it is a mirror image of itself.

7 Draw a 3 point border around the diagram on the Call routing slide.

8 Duplicate the first slide and move the copy to become the last slide.

9 Remove slide numbers from the footer of all slides.

10 Save as **Office Procedures Version 2**.

11 Produce a screenshot of Slide Sorter view, add your name and print. Label it **Printout 3**.

12 Set the show up to loop continuously.

13 Save the slideshow as a show called **Office Show** that will run without having to open PowerPoint first. You will demonstrate this later. Close **Office Show**.

14 Open **Office Procedures Version 2** and remove the timings and sound.

15 Save as **Office Procedures Version 3**.

16 Print slides 6 and 7 as handouts, two to a page in Pure black and white format. Label it **Printout 4**.

17 Produce a screenshot of all filenames used in this assignment. Label it **Printout 5**.

18 Close all open presentations and close PowerPoint.

19 Demonstrate **Office Show** to your tutor.

Write down answers to the following:

20 When might you use a looped slideshow?

21 Why should you be careful if using images from the Internet?

Appendix

Text files are required for some sections. The following should be keyed in using word or text processing software such as Word or WordPad and saved into a new folder called **Text files**.

Section 5

COUNTRIES
Key in the following text as set out below. Save it as **Countries**.

Northern Hemisphere
North America
United States
Canada
Europe
United Kingdom
Spain
Southern Hemisphere
South America
Argentina
Venezuela
Australasia
Australia
New Zealand

COLDS AND FLU
Key in the following text as set out below. Save it as **Colds and Flu**.

Symptoms
Colds
Symptoms
Tickly/sore throat
Runny nose and sneezing
Watering eyes
Headache and temperature
Flu
Symptoms
Headache
Sore throat
High temperature
Fatigue
Tiredness
Weakness
Muscular aches

PREVENTION AND TREATMENT

Key in the following text as set out below. Save it as **Prevention And Treatment**.

COLDS AND FLU

Prevention
A healthy diet that contains plenty of vegetables and fruit and a lifestyle that includes exercise can reduce the chances of catching colds and flu. Those who are at risk from stress are likely to have a weaker immune system and more likely to catch colds. The effects of flu are more serious and can be fatal in the vulnerable or elderly.

Treatment for Colds
Stay in the warm and drink plenty of fluids. Cold remedies from the chemist can help to relieve the symptoms of the cold but will not cure it.

Treatment for Flu
Bed rest for two or three days and drink plenty of fluids. It can take a good week to recover and many people feel very tired for another week or so after that.

CAR SECURITY

Key in the following text as set out below. Save it as **Car Security**.

Park carefully
Out and About
Park in a busy area
Park in a well lit area
Park in a patrolled car park
At home
Park in a garage or driveway
Car Security
Lock doors every time you leave your car
Do not leave valuables on display
Never leave vehicle documents in your car
Never leave keys in the ignition, even in the garage
Etch windows with your registration number
If the car is without an immobiliser, use a steering wheel lock

Section 8

Key in the following text as set out below. Save it as **Newburch Motors**.

Spring Sales Drive
Local advertising campaign
Open day
Special Deals
New model
Advertising Campaign
Newspapers
Radio
Regional TV
Flyer in local free papers
Open Day
Test drives
Refreshments
Freebies
Children's Corner
Current Sales Structure
Proposed Sales Structure A
Proposed Sales Structure B
Branch Sales For Last Quarter
Percentage Sales

Section 10

Key in the following text and save as set out below. Save it as **Procedures**.

1 E-mail etiquette
Always enter a subject line
Be concise
Do not SHOUT, i.e. use capitals
Do not spam all users
Think before you press Send
2 Managing e-mails
Set aside time daily to deal with messages
Delete messages regularly
Create a folder system for storage
3 Voicemail
4 Recording a greeting
State your name
Request detailed message to be left
State when you will return calls
Instructions for urgent callers
Change greeting when off premises
5 Leaving a message
State your name
Date and time
Short detailed Message
State number and repeat

Solutions

Section 1 Presentation graphics – basics

Practise your skills 1.1

Applications Software

An Introduction

Different types

- Word Processing
- Spreadsheet
- Database
- Desktop Publishing
- Presentation Graphics

Word Processing

- Working mainly with text
- Letters
- Memos
- Reports
- Lists
- Tables

Spreadsheets

- Working with numbers
- Budgets
- Invoices
- Accounts
- Charts

Databases

- Storing and organising data
- Searching
- Sorting
- Listing
- Reporting

Desktop Publishing

- Working with text and graphics
- Posters
- Leaflets
- Advertisements
- Newsletters
- Booklets

Presentation Graphics

- For presenting information
- Text
- Images
- Shapes
- Effects

Presented by

Your name

Databases

- Storing and organising data
- Searching
- Sorting
- Listing
- Reporting

Presentation Graphics

- For presenting information
- Text
- Images
- Shapes
- Effects

Practise your skills 1.2

City & Guilds

e-Quals for IT Users

Level 3 – Advanced Diploma for IT Users

- IT Principles
- Word Processing
- Spreadsheets
- Desk Top Publishing
- Integrated Applications
- Web Site Design
- Relational Databases

Level 2 – Diploma for IT Users

- Word Processing
- Spreadsheets
- Databases
- Using the Internet
- Presentation Graphics
- Computerised Accounts
- Desk Top Publishing
- Integrated Applications
- Multi media
- Web Site Design

Level 1 – Certificate for IT Users

- IT Principles
- Word processing
- Spreadsheets
- Databases
- Using the Internet
- Presentation Graphics
- E-Mail
- Desk Top Publishing

City & Guilds

e-Quals for IT Users

Level 1 – Certificate for IT Users

- IT Principles
- Word processing
- Spreadsheets
- Databases
- Using the Internet
- Presentation Graphics
- E-Mail
- Desk Top Publishing

Level 2 – Diploma for IT Users

- Word Processing
- Spreadsheets
- Databases
- Using the Internet
- Presentation Graphics
- Computerised Accounts
- Desk Top Publishing
- Integrated Applications
- Multi media
- Web Site Design

Level 3 – Advanced Diploma for IT Users

- IT Principles
- Word Processing
- Spreadsheets
- Desk Top Publishing
- Integrated Applications
- Web Site Design
- Relational Databases

Presented by

Your name

1 ☐ City & Guilds
   e-Quals for IT Users

2 ☐ Level 1 – Certificate for IT Users
   - IT Principles
   - Word processing
   - Spreadsheets
   - Databases
   - Using the Internet
   - Presentation Graphics
   - E-Mail
   - Desk Top Publishing

3 ☐ Level 2 – Diploma for IT Users
   1 - Word Processing
      - Spreadsheets
      - Databases
      - Using the Internet
      - Presentation Graphics
      - Computerised Accounts

   2 - Desk Top Publishing
      - Integrated Applications
      - Multi media
      - Web Site Design

4 ☐ Level 3 – Advanced Diploma for IT Users
   - IT Principles
   - Word Processing
   - Spreadsheets
   - Desk Top Publishing
   - Integrated Applications
   - Web Site Design
   - Relational Databases

5 ☐ Presented by
   Your name

Check your knowledge

1 These are layouts provided with ready-made placeholders for text, clip art and other objects.

2 Objects such as headings will be in the same position on each slide, making a smoother presentation. Placeholders are formatted to particular fonts and sizes.

3 Select a slide. Choose Slide Layout from the Format menu and select the required option.

4 Either click on the Normal View icon ▣ or double-click on a slide.

5 Hold the Control key down and click on each slide that needs to be selected.

Section 2 Master slides

Practise your skills 2.1

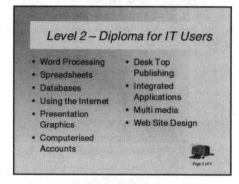

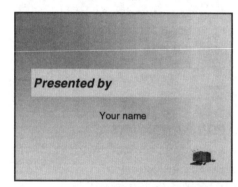

Check your knowledge

1 A Master slide is used to set the font, font size and position of the placeholders upon which each slide is based. Logos and graphics can be placed on the Master and backgrounds chosen. Changes made to the Master will be applied automatically to existing slides and to any new slides.

2 Consider the legibility of the text against the background.

3 Ensure the text is large enough to read because slides are normally shown on a large screen, to an audience who may be viewing from a distance. Ensure text is clear and large enough to read. Avoid fancy fonts. Text colours should be chosen with care to ensure slides can be read easily, particularly when a coloured background is used

4 Locking aspect ratio ensures the object will stay in its original proportion and not become distorted.

5 Update automatically – displays the current date.
Fixed – you must key in the date required.

Consolidation 1

 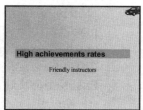 

 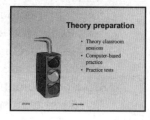 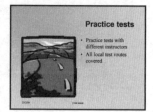

1 🗀 **Smarts Driving School**

2 🗀 **High achievements rates**

Friendly instructors

3 🗀 **Services**

- Driving lessons
- Intensive courses
- Theory preparation
- Practice tests
- Advanced driving
- Motorway driving
- Refresher courses

4 🗀 **Intensive courses**

- One week all day
- Two weeks half day
- Individual programmes
- Test at the end

5 🗀 **Theory preparation**

- Theory classroom sessions
- Computer-based practice
- Practice tests

6 🗀 **Practice tests**

- Practice tests with different instructors
- All local test routes covered

7 🗀 **Other courses**

- Advanced driving – preparation for the Advanced driving test
- Motorway driving – minimum two half day sessions
- Refresher courses – for those whose driving is a little rusty

Section 3 Templates

Practise your skills 3.2

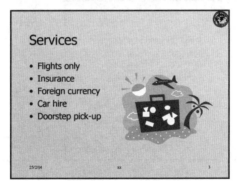

Check your knowledge

1 Design templates are formatted presentation designs each with their own colour scheme and decorative graphics ready to complete. The designs include background colours, fonts, font colours and bullet styles. If applied to an existing presentation the new design overwrites the formatting applied to the Master slides.

2 If any mistakes have been made they will appear every time the template is used.

3 They save time because text and/or graphics can be included on a template so that they are already in place when you come to use it. This means that users can concentrate on the content of the presentation. Templates also ensure consistency – each presentation will have the same 'look'.

4 Apart from the reasons given for number 3, a house style template will ensure that everyone in an organisation follows the same style and layout. This is particularly important if, for example, presentations are to be shown to clients.

5 The file extension of a presentation is .ppt and a template is .pot.

Section 4 Working with text

Practise your skills 4.1

_____
_____
_____
_____
_____
_____

_____
_____
_____
_____
_____
_____
_____
_____

_____
_____
_____
_____
_____
_____
_____

Check your knowledge

1 To draw attention to text, to give variety and interest to a slide.

2 Using the text box tool, click on the slide and key in text, or drag and draw a text box.

3 The text in click and type text boxes does not word wrap. In drag and draw text boxes it does.

4

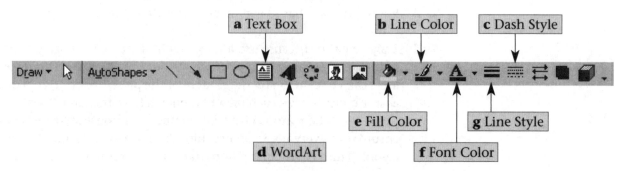

Section 5 Text from other sources

Practise your skills 5.1

1 ▢ **Winter Ailments**

Symptoms

2 ▢ **Colds**

- Symptoms
  - Tickly/sore throat
  - Runny nose and sneezing
  - Watering eyes
  - Headache and temperature

3 ▢ **Flu**

- Symptoms
  - Headache
  - Sore throat
  - High temperature
  - Fatigue
    - Tiredness
    - Weakness
    - Muscular aches

Practise your skills 5.2

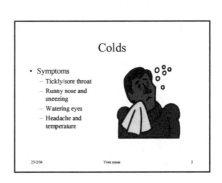

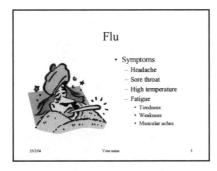

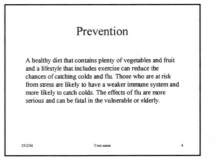

Check your knowledge

1 The Promote button ⬅ makes a point more important.

The Demote button ➡ makes a point less important.

2 Bullets are useful for presenting facts in a list. Sometimes one bullet point will have a further list of sub-items which are less important than the main item.

3 To make a paragraph stand out from the rest of the text.

4 From text files on your computer, from disk, CD or from the Internet.

5 Copyright means that the creator or owner has the right to control who can make copies and how their work can be used. You cannot use copyrighted work without permission. This applies to text and graphics.

Consolidation 2

1 ⬚ **Smarts Driving School**
    Keep it safe

2 ⬚ **Park carefully**
    ◇ Out and About
        – Park in a busy area
        – Park in a well lit area
        – Park in a patrolled car park
    ◇ At home
        – Park in a garage or driveway

3 ⬚ **Car Security**
    ◇ Lock doors every time you leave your car
    ◇ Do not leave valuables on display
    ◇ Never leave vehicle documents in your car
    ◇ Never leave keys in the ignition, even in the garage
    ◇ Etch windows with your registration number
    ◇ If the car is without an immmobiliser, use a steering wheel lock

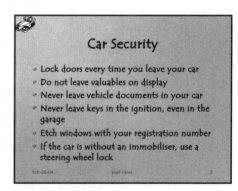

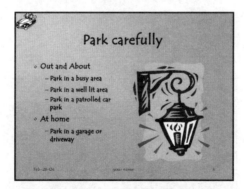

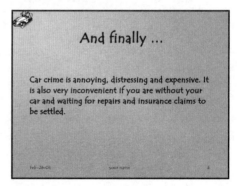

Section 6 Graphical shapes

Practise your skills 6.1

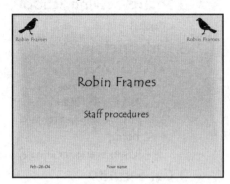

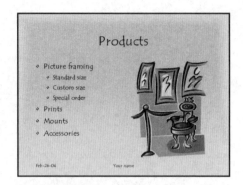

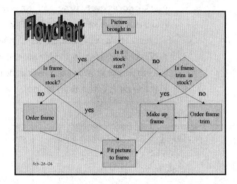

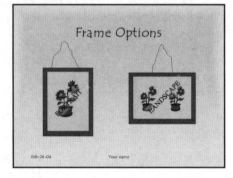

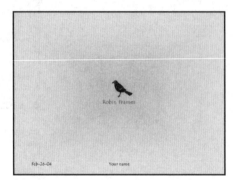

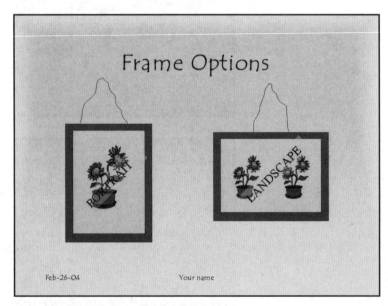

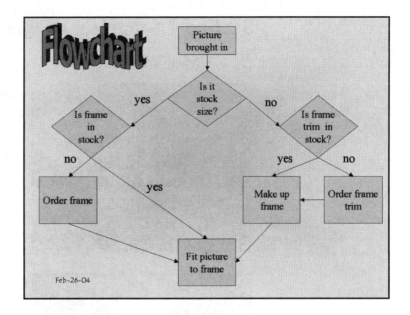

Practise your skills 6.2

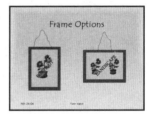

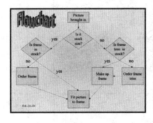

Check your knowledge

1   Hold down the Shift key as you draw.
2   Select AutoShapes on the Drawing toolbar and then Stars and Banners.
    Position the pointer over each shape until the tip appears telling you the
    shape you want.
3   Each layer can be handled and formatted separately. Layers can be re-
    arranged by reordering the layers bringing one object to the front of the
    pile or sending another to the back of the pile.
4   So they can then be moved, resized or copied as one object. This is much
    easier than dealing with lots of single objects. If you need to change one
    object within a group, then you can easily ungroup them.
5   Ungroup it, then regroup it again.

Section 7 Graphical images

Practise your skills 7.1

Practise your skills 7.2

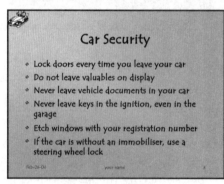

Check your knowledge

1 Create your own using a digital camera or scanner, purchase them on CD-ROM or find them in PowerPoint ClipArt Gallery. Find them on the internet or on your college intranet.

2 If you are using images, especially for commercial purposes, they should be copyright-free unless you have permission to use them. You could break copyright law.

3 Either right-click on an image, save it and then insert it. Alternatively, right-click to copy the image and then paste it into the presentation. Using the first method means that you have an image file saved for future use. With copying and pasting you do not.

4 Drag a corner handle.

5 It is the cropping tool – used to cut off unwanted sides of an image.

Section 8 Charts

Practise your skills 8.1

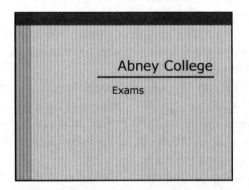

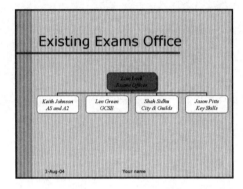

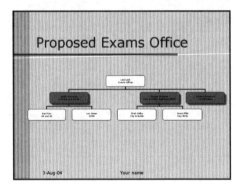

Practise your skills 8.2

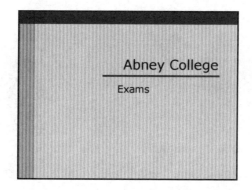

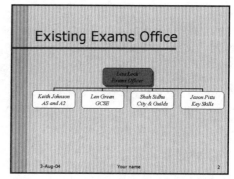

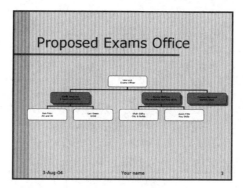

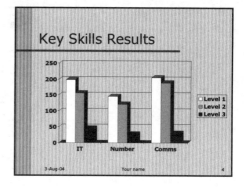

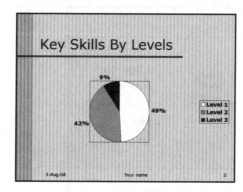

Check your knowledge

1 Organisation charts and charts or graphs.

2 It is much easier to read and understand at a glance than a table of numbers.

3 Bar or column – used to show comparison between sets of numbers using horizontal bars or vertical columns.

4 Line – trends over a period of time are shown by drawing connecting lines between points.

5 Pie – percentage values are represented as slices of a pie.

Consolidation 3

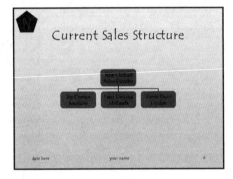

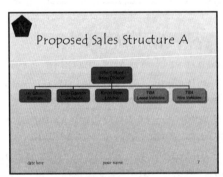

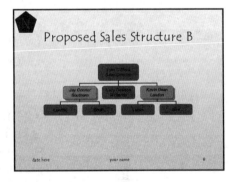

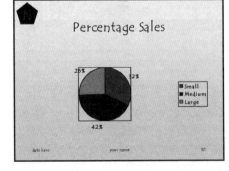

Section 9 Special effects

Practise your skills 9.1

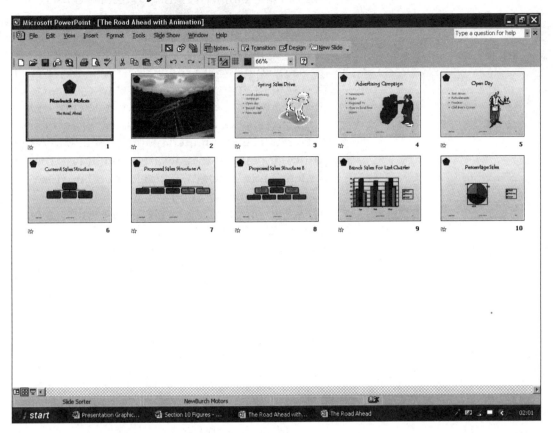

Practise your skills 9.2

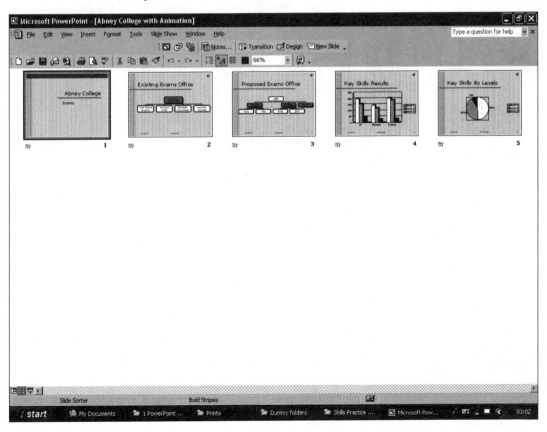

Check your knowledge

1 Slide transition effects.
2 Custom animation. It is used to display objects on slides one after the other. Bullet points appear one at a time. Chart categories can be made to appear one at a time. The order of objects can be changed.
3 Animated pictures (gif), sound (midi) and video (avi) files.
4 The two terms are fairly interchangeable. However a presentation is likely to be controlled manually by a speaker who advances each slide when he or she is ready. A slideshow might better describe a series of slides that are set to run automatically without the need for anyone to control them.
5 They can be useful if used sparingly and with care to introduce a particular point or to draw attention. If not, they may detract from the content of the slides. A recorded sound or video file could be useful, however too many sound and animation effects can be irritating and if not set up properly might play at the wrong moment or play for too long or not play at all when required.
6 The same points apply. A video clip could be useful though, as could sound in the form of a recorded commentary or even an unobtrusive soundtrack.

Section 10 Finishing touches

Practise your skills 10.1

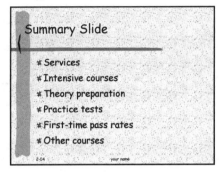

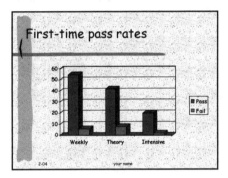

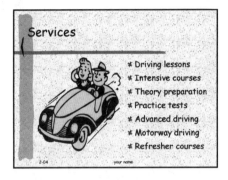

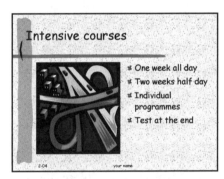

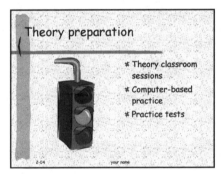

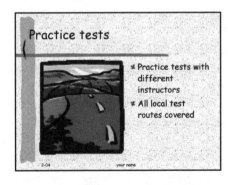

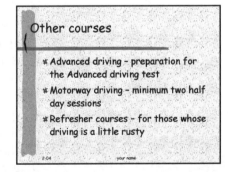

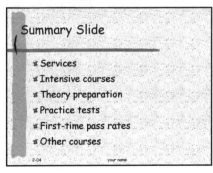

Practise your skills 10.2

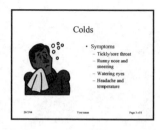

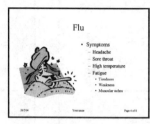

Check your knowledge

1 Colours can look muddy and patterns do not always print as seen onscreen. Any colour used to distinguish, say, segments of a pie chart or parts of a diagram, will not show.

2 Summary slides are created from the titles of selected slides and are useful at the start of a presentation as an introduction and/or at the end to recap.

3 Sometimes you may not want to use a slide in a particular presentation but you do not want to delete it as it will be needed later.

4 Slide Sorter view and Outline view. It is easier to do in Slide Sorter view.

5 1 – Rehearse timings, 2 – Select Slide Transition from the Slideshow menu and set a time.

6 A looped and time slideshow runs automatically on its own and might be used for an exhibition or a college open evening.

7 A manually run presentation with a mouse pointer would be used by a speaker giving a talk.

8 So it can be used on a computer without PowerPoint, for example on a client's premises.

9 Pack and Go.

10 Save it as a file type PowerPoint Show.

Practice assignment

Worked examples to Tasks A–C

  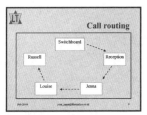

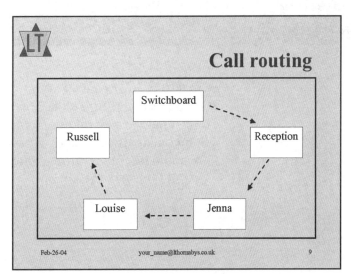

At busy times calls not answered within 5 rings will be automatically re-routed following this diagram.

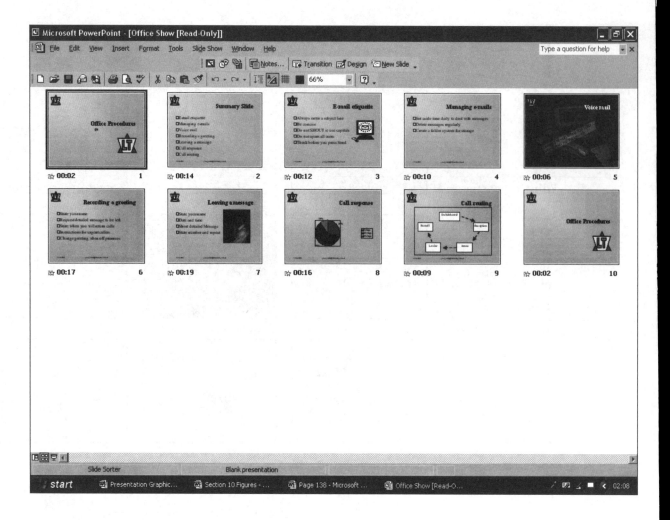

Answers to Task C

20 A looped and time slideshow runs automatically on its own and might be used for an exhibition or a college open evening.

21 If you are using images, especially for commercial purposes, they should be copyright-free unless you have permission to use them. You could break copyright law.

Outcomes matching guide

Outcome 1 Create and save a new presentation/slideshow template

Practical activities

1	Load presentation graphics software and select a blank template	All sections
2	Edit the master and/or title slides to • change the background graphic/colours • change default text-attributes: size, font, colour • add footers, page numbering, dates etc. • change default slide layout	Section 2 onwards Section 4 onwards Section 2 onwards Section 2 onwards Section 2 onwards
3	Save new template in an appropriate location	Section 3

Underpinning knowledge

1	Describe the benefits of templates in standardising house styles of presentation	Section 3
2	Describe the different date, filename and numbering formats available	Sections 2, 3, 10

Outcome 2 Add text to a presentation/slideshow from various sources, and control its attributes

Practical activities

1	Insert text boxes and add text to presentation	Section 4
2	Cut and paste text into Outline view • from a text processor • from a web browser	Section 5
3	Change text box properties to permit autowrap, auto-size, text-rotate	Section 4
4	Change text box properties: border style, weight, background	Section 4
5	Import selected text from another application or the internet using cut and paste	Section 5
6	Check text for spelling, adding to the dictionary where appropriate	Section 1
7	Change text attributes: font, size, colour	Sections 1, 2, 4
8	Use indented and bulleted text	Section 5 All sections
9	Use graphical text where appropriate	Section 4

Underpinning knowledge

1	Identify sources of text and graphics that may be inserted into a presentation	Section 4
2	Describe copyright constraints on the importing of text and graphics from external sources	Section 5 Section 7
3	Describe the use of text boxes and their properties	Section 4
4	Identify criteria for the selection of text attributes (size, colour, font etc.)	Section 2
5	Identify criteria for indenting and suitably bulleting text	Section 4
6	Identify criteria for the use of graphical text	Section 4

Outcome 3 Add graphical objects to a presentation/slideshow from various sources, and control their attributes		
Practical activities		
1	Insert images from disk/network drive, CD, internet/intranet	Section 7
2	Insert graphical objects from files	Section 8
3	Create graphical chart objects	Section 8
4	Place and resize objects in slides	Sections 1, 2, 6
5	Duplicate and delete objects	Sections 3, 6, 10
6	Copy objects to other slides	Section 6
7	Insert pre-defined shapes and add additional lines and arrows/connectors	Section 6
8	Add text to pre-defined shapes	Section 6
9	Modify colour and lines for pre-defined shapes	Section 6
10	Group sets of graphical objects to create diagrams, eg organisational diagrams from graphical primitives	Section 6
Underpinning knowledge		
1	Describe sources of graphical files • Picture and image libraries • Computer-drawn images • Scanned images	Section 7
2	Describe the differences between the import process for an object and a graphic file from disk, network drive or CD-ROM, and from an object in an internet browser	Section 7
3	Identify the available chart objects	Section 8
4	Describe the advantages of grouping and ungrouping objects	Section 6
Outcome 4 Add animation and multimedia objects to a presentation/slideshow		
Practical activities		
1	Place sound objects in slides	Section 9
2	Place animated objects in slides	Section 9
3	Animate sequences of graphical or text insertions on to slides	Section 9
4	Control activation of animated/multimedia objects using • timing control • pointer control	Sections 9, 10
5	Control inserted sounds so they are the background for multiple slides	Section 9
Underpinning knowledge		
1	Identify types of multimedia file format suited to the hardware and software available	Section 9
2	Describe text and graphical sequence animation options and methods available	Section 9
3	Describe advantages and disadvantages of multimedia inserts in a slideshow	Section 9
4	Describe advantages and disadvantages of multimedia inserts in a slideshow	Section 9

Outcome 5 Refine and standardise the appearance of slides for presentation		
Practical activities		
1	Set page margins, tabs and indents	Section 4
2	Activate the ruler and guidelines	Section 4
3	Position and align text and graphical objects • dynamically using the ruler • by setting positional properties	Section 4 Section 7
4	Group text as annotations as with graphical objects	Section 6
5	Reposition and resize grouped objects	Section 6
6	Use layers to order objects on at least three layers with transparent and opaque backgrounds	Section 6
7	Rotate, mirror and invert simple and complex/compound objects	Section 6
Underpinning knowledge		
1	Describe the benefits of using layers to order object	Section 6
2	Describe the benefits of grouping and ungrouping objects	Section 6
Outcome 6 Produce hard copy from and viewer versions of a presentation/slideshow		
Practical activities		
1	Print a single slide from the presentation	Section 1
2	Print the whole presentation with multiple/single slides per page: • as handouts • with notes	Section 1 Section 10
3	Save a presentation/slideshow as a package complete with viewer software	Section 10
Underpinning knowledge		
1	Describe the problems associate with printing colour slides on a monochrome printer	Section 10
2	Describe the reasons why a presentation has to be packaged with a viewer for use away from the machine on which it was created	Section 10
Outcome 7 Order slides, select transitions and run slideshows		
Practical activities		
1	Use a slide viewer or sorter to: • duplicate and delete existing slides • put sequences of slides into order	Section 10 Section 1, 6, 8, 10
2	Arrange suitable transition actions between slides	Section 9
3	Select types of transition between slides: • Timed • Pointer-controlled	Sections 9, 10
4	Create pointer-controlled presentations with at least ten slides with suitable title and summary slides	Section 10
5	Run presentations using a pointer device to control slide transition	Section 9
6	Create looped, timed slideshows with at least five slides, tested for appropriate length of appearance of each slide	Section 10
7	Run looped slideshows	Section 10

Underpinning knowledge		
1	Describe the use of different views of the presentation in sequencing the slides	Sections 1, 10
2	Identify advantages and disadvantages of different forms of transition	Section 9
3	Identify appropriate occasions for the use of presentation graphics software • illustrating talks/arguments (eg pointer-controlled) • automatic exhibition slideshows (eg looped, timed)	Section 10
4	Identify suitable title framing for presentations	Section 10
5	Identify suitable timings for slides of different content	Section 10

Quick reference guide

Action	Button	Menu	Keyboard
Animation		Slideshow Custom Animation (not Slide Sorter view)	
AutoShapes	AutoShapes ▾ on Drawing toolbar		
Background		Format – Background	
Bold	**B**	Format – Font	Ctrl + B
Bullets	≔	Format – Bullets and Numbering	
Cancel			Esc
Centre align	≡	Format – Alignment	Ctrl + E
Change case		Format – Change case	
Change slide layout		Format – Slide Layout	
Chart effects	In Normal view select the chart – select Slideshow menu – Custom Animation – Add Effect – select chart object in task pane – dropdown arrow – Effect options		
Close or Exit		File – Close or Exit	Alt + F4
Copy	🗐	Edit – Copy	Ctrl + C
Copy a slide	In Slide Sorter view – select Slide – Copy – paste in new position or Insert – duplicate slide		
Custom animation	In Slide or Normal view – select Slide – Slideshow menu – Custom Animation. Check each object to be animated		
Cut	✂	Edit – Cut	Ctrl + X
Demote (Indent)	➡		Tab key
Design template		Format – Apply Design Template	
End of line			End
Exit or Close		File – Close or Exit	Alt + F4
Flip	Draw – Rotate or Flip (For clip art – Ungroup and Group first)		
Font	Arial ▾	Format – Font	
Font size	12 ▾	Format – Font	
Format objects		Format – Object/ AutoShape/ Text Box/ Picture	
Footer		View – Header and Footer	

Group		Drawing toolbar – Draw – Group	
Guides		View – Guides Ctrl and drag for a new guide	
Hide a slide	in Slide Sorter view	Slideshow – Hide Slide	
Indent (Demote)			Tab key
Insert clip art	from Drawing toolbar	Insert – Picture – ClipArt	
Insert new slide		Insert – New slide	
Insert Picture		Insert – Picture – From File	
Insert sound	Insert – Movies and Sound – Sound from Clip Organizer (or from File)		
Italics	I	Format – Font	Ctrl + I
Justify		Format – Alignment	Ctrl + J
Left align		Format – Alignment	Ctrl + L
Line spacing		Format – Line Spacing	
Master slide		View – Master – Slide Master	
New presentation		File – New	Ctrl + N
New slide		Insert – New Slide	
Normal view		View – Normal	
Numbering		Format – Bullets and Numbering	
Open file		File – Open	Ctrl + O
Order		Drawing toolbar – Draw – Order	
Paper size/orientation		File – Page Setup	
Paste		Edit – Paste	Ctrl + V
Print		File – Print	Ctrl + P
Promote			
Redo		Edit – Redo	
Rehearse timings	in Slide Sorter view	Slideshow – Rehearse Timings	
Right align		Format – Alignment	Ctrl + R
Rotate	Draw – Rotate	Format – Object/ AutoShape/ Text Box/ Picture	
Ruler		View – Ruler	

Save	💾	File – Save	Ctrl + S
Save As		File – Save As	F12
Select All (in a text box)		Edit – Select All	Ctrl + A
Shadow	**S**	Format – Font	
Slide order (change)	In Slide Sorter view – drag slide to new position On Slide/Outline tab – drag slide icon to new position		
Slideshow view	🖥	View – Slideshow	F5
Slide Sorter view	⊞	View – Slide Sorter	
Slide transition	**⟱ Transition** (in Slide Sorter view)	Slideshow – Slide Transition	
Sound		Insert – Movies and Sound	
Spellcheck	ABC✓	Tools – Spelling and Grammar	F7
Start of line			Home
Summary slide	📑 in Slide Sorter view – select Slides first (use Control and click the slides whose titles you want to use)		
Text box	📄	Insert – Text Box	
Underline	**U**	Format – Font	Ctrl + U
Undo	↩	Edit – Undo	
Ungroup		Drawing toolbar – Draw – Ungroup	
View options	▦ ⊞ 🖥	View menu – Select	

Select text

To select:	Method
One word	Double-click on word (also selects the following space)
Several words	Press and drag the I-beam across several words and release
A sentence	Hold down **Ctrl**. Click anywhere in sentence
A block of text	Click cursor at start point, hold down **Shift**. Click cursor at end point
To deselect	Click anywhere off the text

Drawing toolbar

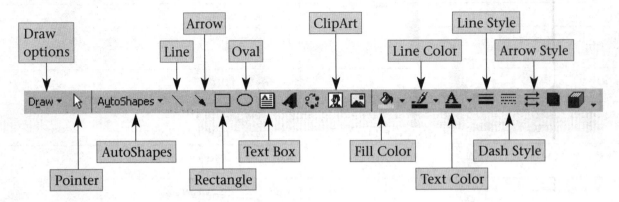

Right mouse button

Clicking the right mouse button provides menu options depending on what you are doing at the time, eg when right-clicked in text, you have Cut, Copy, Paste etc.

Help

For Help at any time, click on the **Help** menu and select **Microsoft PowerPoint Help**. The Office Assistant appears. Type in a question and click on **Search** for a list of possible solutions from which to choose. To turn off the Office Assistant, select **Hide Office Assistant** from the **Help** menu.